Leverage

Leverage

Using PLCs to Promote
Lasting Improvement in Schools

Thomas W. Many

Susan K. Sparks-Many

Foreword by Richard DuFour

CORWIN
A SAGE Company

FOR INFORMATION:

Corwin
A SAGE Company
2455 Teller Road
Thousand Oaks, California 91320
(800) 233-9936
www.corwin.com

SAGE Publications Ltd.
1 Oliver's Yard
55 City Road
London EC1Y 1SP
United Kingdom

SAGE Publications India Pvt. Ltd.
B 1/I 1 Mohan Cooperative Industrial Area
Mathura Road, New Delhi 110 044
India

SAGE Publications Asia-Pacific Pte. Ltd.
3 Church Street
#10-04 Samsung Hub
Singapore 049483

Acquisitions Editor: Dan Alpert
Associate Editor: Kim Greenberg
Editorial Assistant: Cesar Reyes
Project Editor: Veronica Stapleton Hooper
Copy Editor: Cate Huisman
Typesetter: C&M Digitals (P) Ltd.
Proofreader: Wendy Jo Dymond
Indexer: Karen Wiley
Cover Designer: Anupama Krishnan
Marketing Manager: Stephanie Trkay

Printed in the United States of America.

Library of Congress Cataloging-in-Publication Data

Many, Thomas W.
Leverage : using PLCs to promote lasting improvement in schools / Thomas W. Many, Susan K. Sparks-Many; foreword by Richard DuFour.

pages cm
Includes bibliographical references and index.

ISBN 978-1-4522-5957-4 (alk. paper)

1. Professional learning communities—United States. 2. Educational leadership—United States. 3. Educational change—United States. I. Title.

LB1738.M29 2014
370.71′1—dc23   2014020151

This book is printed on acid-free paper.

15 16 17 18 19 10 9 8 7 6 5 4 3 2 1

Contents

Foreword

My career in education is approaching the half-century mark, and during that time I have witnessed an evolving role for principals. In the mid-1970s, when I was appointed to my first principalship, a union leader at the school told me that the staff was looking for a "benevolent dictator." Over time I came to understand he meant I should be benevolent to the staff and a dictator to the kids. I learned that if the kids were well behaved, the teachers were happy, and the central office wasn't receiving parent complaints about the school, I was considered a highly effective principal.

In the mid-1980s I took on my second principalship. By then the effective schools research had established that the elements of effective schooling could neither be brought together nor kept together without strong administrative leadership from the principal. Expectations for the position were growing but remained ambiguous. Principals were urged to be instructional leaders, transformational leaders, servant leaders, strategic leaders, learning leaders, empowering leaders, and moral leaders. What did effective principal leadership look like?

But throughout my 14 years as a principal in two different schools, one thing was crystal clear: I would be busy. I never needed to worry about creating a "to do" list for my job. All I had to do was show up for work, and I would be kept busy all day. There were discipline problems to solve, parent questions to answer, classrooms to observe, faculty concerns to address, conflicts to mediate, central office demands to meet, assemblies to attend, state reports to complete, new programs to implement, committees to chair, and daily logistics to monitor. And as a high school principal, I had the added bonus of receiving lots of advice on improving our athletic program (usually by firing a coach); developing better ways to select cheerleaders or determine the lead in the musical; providing more attention to the arts or a particular sport; and determining whether a textbook, a novel, a play, or an article in our student newspaper was appropriate for students.

When I read the following job description for principals in 1998, it struck a chord:

Wanted: a miracle worker who can do more with less, pacify rival groups, endure chronic second-guessing, tolerate low levels of support, process large volumes of paper, and work double shifts (75 nights a year). He or she will have carte blanche to innovate but cannot spend much money, replace any personnel, or upset any constituency.

Fast-forward to today, and the challenges of the principalship are infinitely more complex than those I faced. An accurate job description for the contemporary principalship would need to be extended: As the principal of a school, you would be held accountable for the following:

- Implementing the most comprehensive curriculum reform in American history *with fidelity* while encouraging creativity and innovation among your staff.
- Devoting the majority of your day to monitoring instruction in the classroom while maintaining an open door policy and being immediately accessible to all stakeholders.
- Building consensus for change while assertively demanding change based on the most promising strategies for improving schools.
- Maintaining a relentless focus on priorities while tending to the 21 specific tasks your position demands.
- Building strong parent partnerships while buffering your staff from parental concerns or complaints.
- Achieving a goal that has never been reached in the United States (high levels of learning for all students) while coping with cuts in staffing and funding.

Through this cacophony of mixed signals, Tom Many and Susan-Sparks Many present a comparatively simple message to principals. They assert the following:

1. You play a key role in creating the conditions for effective schooling and improved student learning.

2. It is beyond the capacity of any individual to meet all of the demands of the contemporary principalship.

3. There are specific actions and improvement strategies available to you that are far more effective in having a positive impact on student achievement than others.

4. To be effective as a principal you must focus your effort and energies on these most impactful actions and strategies.

Although the authors take pains to establish the solid research base behind each of these assertions, almost all contemporary educators would agree with these statements based on their everyday observations. As each of these statements builds up the next, clearly it would just make sense that principals should concentrate on readily identifiable, high-leverage strategies for improving their schools. But, alas, as Voltaire observed, "Common sense is not so common."

So the authors set out to accomplish several objectives in this book. They hope to persuade principals that their effectiveness will depend to a large extent on their ability to focus their efforts on high-leverage strategies. They explicitly and directly articulate what those high-leverage strategies are. They provide examples, tools, and templates to help principals move forward with the strategies. And, very important, they create a moral imperative for doing the right work.

One of the best features of *Leverage* is its lack of ambiguity. The authors don't simply suggest high-leverage strategies exist; they clearly and repeatedly stipulate exactly what those strategies entail. Their message to principals is straightforward:

- Organize your staff into collaborative teams.
- Ensure that teams are providing students with a guaranteed and viable curriculum, unit by unit.
- Ensure that teams are monitoring student learning on an ongoing basis through a balanced assessment process that includes a team-developed common formative assessment.
- Ensure that teams use the results of the assessments to give students who struggle access to a schoolwide system of intervention that guarantees they will receive additional time and support for learning in a way that is timely, directive, and diagnostic and that occurs during the school day.
- Ensure that teams provide students who are already highly proficient with opportunities for enrichment and extension of their learning.
- Ensure that teams use the results from the assessment process to inform and improve the professional practice of both individual members and the entire team.
- Create the schedules, structures, and protocols that support this process of continuous improvement.
- Sustain your focus on these key elements, and celebrate incremental progress.
- In short, *Leverage* calls upon educators to transform their schools and districts into Professional Learning Communities, not in name but in practice.

There is a tendency in the field of education to make the simple complex. The key to effective communication, however, is to make the complex elegantly simple. Many and Sparks-Many have done just that and thus have made a significant contribution to the literature on Professional Learning Communities.

I urge principals to study the message of this book. The authors are absolutely correct in pointing out that the question facing the contemporary principal is not "Will I work hard?" You can be assured: You will work hard. The real questions are, "Will I focus on the right work?" and "Will I then sustain that focus when not everyone is supportive, when we are confronted with the inevitable obstacles of substantive change, when my well-intentioned efforts are met with resistance, and when, as James McGregor Burns said, 'I am receiving far less than universal affection?'" No book can give principals the courage to lead the changes that are necessary to meet the demands being placed upon educators. But for those individuals who have the courage, the book provides the guideposts they need for moving forward.

Dr. Richard DuFour
Educational Author and Consultant

Preface

Hundreds of books have defined the attributes, qualities, and traits of great leaders. Of these, dozens have been written that describe the dimensions of effective leadership in schools. These authors have distilled the global theories of school-level leadership into contextual applications for anyone aspiring to make a positive, significant, and lasting impact on the lives of students who attend his or her school.

For nearly 20 years, leading experts in the field of education have pointed to Professional Learning Communities as the most effective strategy for improving schools. The importance of a guaranteed and viable curriculum, a balanced and coherent system of assessments, and school-wide, systematic pyramids of intervention are not up for debate. Neither is the idea that teachers are most effective when they work together on collaborative teams. The consensus is clear. As Milbrey McLaughlin said, "The most promising strategy for sustained, substantive school improvement is building the capacity of school personnel to function as a professional learning community" (1995).

This book is focused specifically on aspects of leadership related to the principal's role in leading a Professional Learning Community. It is our belief that learning is the fundamental purpose of schools and that leaders best meet our collective commitment to the children we serve through the successful implementation of Professional Learning Communities in every classroom, every school, and every district across the land.

In schools functioning as Professional Learning Communities, the work is deeply rooted in best practice and is grounded in optimistic certainty. Because we believe that all children can learn, they do. Because we believe working together in collaborative teams is more effective, it is. Because we believe that every child in every school deserves our best efforts every day, we provide learning opportunities characterized by limitless possibilities for our children.

When we believe in ourselves, our colleagues, and our community, we can make a difference for our children. By continuing to work together, we can create the kind of schools that make a positive and lasting difference for all our children.

Acknowledgments

We would first like to acknowledge the support, guidance, and encouragement of our dear friends and mentors Rick and Becky DuFour. You inspire us with your limitless energy and steadfast commitment.

Next, we want to thank the dedicated and passionate educators we have met. The premise for this book, developed over time, is the result of your questions that challenge us to be practical, concrete, and grounded. You help us translate theory into practice.

We want to recognize our partners at Texas Elementary Principals and Supervisors Association (TEPSA). We thank you for providing us with a platform to explore these ideas and the opportunity to share our thinking around best practice and school improvement with principals.

We appreciate Charl Lee Sauer, Duncan Harrison, and Cate Huisman. We thank them for their feedback, support, and technical expertise during the writing process to help refine our thinking and add clarity.

We are grateful for Dan Alpert and the entire Corwin team. We thank you for believing in the powerful role principals and teacher leaders play in Professional Learning Communities. You have been wonderful guides in what has been a tremendous learning experience.

And finally, we want to express our gratitude to our children: Beth and John, Abbie and Irish, Ben, and Ali. We feel blessed, and every day you remind us of why we do this work and the fact that we can make a difference in the world.

PUBLISHER'S ACKNOWLEDGMENTS

Corwin gratefully acknowledges the contributions of the following reviewers:

Virginia E. Kelsen, PhD
Principal
Rancho Cucamonga High School
Rancho Cucamonga, CA

Alice L. Manus, PhD
Vice Principal
Soldan International Studies High School
St. Louis, Missouri

Douglas Gordon Hesbol, EdD
School Administrator
Laraway CCSD 70C
Joliet, IL

Deborah R. Jackson
Principal
Fairfax County Public Schools
McLean, VA

About the Authors

Dr. Thomas W. Many, former superintendent of schools in Kildeer Countryside Community Consolidated School District 96 in Buffalo Grove, Illinois, works with teachers, administrators, school boards, parents, and other stakeholders on organizational leadership, implementation and change, and Professional Learning Communities strategies and concepts. Tom has proved to be a great resource to schools and has special insight into the importance of the principal's role in ensuring that all students learn to high levels.

His long and distinguished career includes 20 years of experience as a school superintendent. He also served as a classroom teacher, learning center director, curriculum supervisor, principal, and assistant superintendent. A dedicated Professional Learning Communities practitioner, Dr. Many is a compelling and sought-after speaker and writer who has published more than 40 books and articles, most notably as coauthor of *Learning by Doing: A Handbook for Professional Learning Communities at Work* with Rick DuFour, Becky DuFour, and Bob Eaker.

Susan K. Sparks-Many has worked in education for 30 years as a teacher, staff developer, and leader. She retired as executive director of the Front Range BOCES (Boards of Cooperative Educational Services) for Teacher Leadership, where she served 19 metro area school districts and the School of Education and Human Development at the University of Colorado Denver. She has provided training in collaborative teams and Professional Learning Communities and is known for her conflict resolution and communication skills. Susan currently provides facilitation services in schools, government entities, and not-for-profit organizations. Her areas of expertise include consensus building, contract negotiations, and community organizing.

Susan earned a bachelor of arts and teaching certification from Western State College of Colorado and a master of arts and administrative license from the University of Northern Colorado. She lives in Broomfield, Colorado, with her husband, Tom, and her daughter, Ali.

Introduction

The overarching framework for this book reflects the belief that as principals become more knowledgeable about the strategies that have the greatest impact on teaching and learning—and if they focus their time, energy, and attention on successfully implementing those strategies—then teaching and learning will improve.

In many ways, what we are asking of principals is no different from what we ask of teachers when they power and prioritize their standards. In that process, teachers identify what is most important for students to learn, and they focus on teaching the standards that provide students with the best chance of achieving the highest levels of learning. Likewise we argue that principals must *power and prioritize their practice.* In order to ensure that all students learn to high levels, principals must identify which strategies have the greatest leverage and focus on implementing those that will have the most significant impact on teaching and learning in their schools.

Our thinking is built around four beliefs. Each one, when considered on its own, has implications for our practice, but when taken together as a set of related propositions, our beliefs build a persuasive argument for encouraging principals to focus their school improvement efforts on a limited number of high-leverage strategies.

FIRST, PRINCIPALS ARE CRITICAL TO THE FUNDAMENTAL PURPOSE OF SCHOOLS

We believe the fundamental purpose of school is learning. The research on this is clear; the relationship between a building principal's leadership and student achievement is unequivocal. Show us an effective school where all students are learning, and we will show you an effective principal working tirelessly to make a difference. Thus, if schools are going to fulfill their fundamental purpose of learning for all, then we must maximize the effectiveness of the principal's role.

SECOND, THE CAPACITY OF THE PRINCIPALSHIP IS AT, OR NEARING, ITS PRACTICAL LIMIT

We believe that while an effective principal is critical to a successful school, the capacity of the principalship is at its practical limit. The job of a building principal has become more and more complex, as seemingly endless expectations are placed on those who serve in that role. If we agree that principals have limited, or at least finite, resources, especially with regard to time, then we must help them become more disciplined with what initiatives they invest their time in and with how they invest their time and why.

THIRD, SOME STRATEGIES HAVE A GREATER IMPACT THAN OTHERS ON TEACHING AND LEARNING

We believe that there has never been a clearer consensus or greater agreement on what schools should do to positively impact student learning. According to Zemelman, Daniels, and Hyde, "There is a strong consensus among seemingly disparate subject matter fields about how kids learn best. Virtually all the authoritative voices and documents in every teaching field are calling for the same things" (2012, p. 3).

FOURTH, THE MOST EFFECTIVE PRINCIPALS FOCUS ON A FEW, IMPACTFUL STRATEGIES

Finally, we believe we must acknowledge that principals are pulled in dozens of directions every day; therefore, it makes sense to help principals prioritize their practice. Given that time in school is so precious, *especially for principals,* it makes sense to identify the strategies that are effective and efficient and to focus our attention on those strategies that have the greatest impact.

The book is organized into three sections. In Section I, we build a case for the importance of the role of principals in promoting higher levels of student learning and suggest that it will be beneficial if we look at what principals are expected to do through the lens of leverage.

Chapter 1 reviews the positive influence an effective principal has on teaching and learning. The chapter makes a case for differentiating the type of leadership behavior that is most important if principals are to maximize their impact on teaching and learning.

Chapter 2 explores the day-to-day reality of the principalship, identifies the factors contributing to an overloaded and unrealistic set of expectations, and offers some alternatives to consider.

Chapter 3 introduces the concept of *leverage*, develops an operational definition of leverage, and provides support for the notion that, while many strategies improve teaching and learning, principals must focus on those that impact teaching and learning most.

Chapter 4 argues that principals can best fulfill their mission of ensuring high levels of learning for all students by focusing their time, energy, and attention on implementing the big ideas of Professional Learning Communities.

In Section II, we provide concrete examples, practical applications, and specific suggestions for principals seeking to identify and implement specific strategies that promote high levels of learning for all.

In Chapters 5, 6, and 7 we explore opportunities where principals can find the leverage points to promote a Focus on Learning, a Collaborative Culture, and a Results Orientation in their schools. Our belief is that if we provide principals with practical and pragmatic examples of the best-known research and evidence-based practices, we can accelerate the implementation of the strategies that make a difference. We know what works. If we can identify a few high-leverage strategies and the associated leverage points within the system, everyone benefits.

Section III highlights strategies principals can use to rekindle, reignite, and reenergize their Professional Learning Communities. In Chapters 8 and 9 we explore ways to clarify what matters most, methods to identify what is nonnegotiable, and techniques for communicating effectively, and we provide some thoughts on how to respond to resistors in productive ways.

Underlying our thinking is the notion that we make the process of improving schools too complicated. Certainly, ensuring that all students learn is a complex task, but it is not complicated. The solutions we seek are simple, not simplistic. To paraphrase Peter Senge (1990), a few small and well-focused actions by a principal can produce significant, enduring improvement in schools.

Section I

The Principal

1

Leadership Matters

No longer is there a question about the effect of leadership on student achievement. Clearly, leadership makes a difference.

—Waters and Cameron (2007, p. 3)

Leadership matters. Principals make a difference. In fact, according to Linda Darling-Hammond, the leadership provided by an effective building principal is second only to the guidance provided by the classroom teachers in impacting student learning. In her study of the principalship, Darling-Hammond notes, "School leadership strongly affects student learning. Principals are central to the task of building schools that promote powerful teaching and learning for all students" (Darling-Hammond & Bransford, 2005, p. 3).

EVIDENCE OF A PRINCIPAL'S IMPACT ON STUDENT LEARNING

For more than 35 years, scholars have built an extensive body of evidence that supports the important role a principal plays in helping students learn. In summarizing their research in 2009, Matthew Militello, Sharon Rallis, and Ellen Goldring documented the extent to which the relationship between student achievement and effective principals has been carefully studied. Militello, Rallis, and Goldring reported that "the skills, knowledge, and dispositions needed by the school principal to improve instruction have been extensively explored by Elmore, 2000, 2002, 2003;

Hallinger & Heck, 1996; Leithwood, Seashore, Louis, Anderson, & Wahlstrom, 2005; Marzano, Waters, & McNulty, 2005" (2009, p. 17). In each case, the authors cited strong support for the role leaders played in improving student achievement. Their conclusion was self-evident: *Leadership matters.*

But it is not just any leadership that matters. As our understanding of school leadership has evolved, other researchers have identified the "specific types of leadership behavior that had an impact on student achievement" (Militello et al., 2009, p. 17). (See also Leithwood & Mascall, 2008; Marks & Printy, 2003; Robinson, Lloyd, & Rowe, 2008.) Over the past three decades, we have come to understand that the *type of leadership* matters.

Other studies identified specific ways effective principals impact student learning. As Militello and colleagues reported,

> Louis and Miles . . . talked about a close, cohesive internal network when describing the relationships among staff members in those high schools that successfully implement change. More recent studies have shown the importance of principal's role in leading professional learning communities or what Militello and Rallis referred to as "communities of practice." (2009, p. 17)

(See also Militello, Schweid, & Carey, 2008; Printy, 2008; and Supovitz & Christman, 2003.) Militello and colleagues found studies that documented the importance of principals

> taking charge of initiatives centered on the core of teaching and learning . . . investigating policies such as student retention . . . and using data to develop new support mechanisms and to implement new teaching and learning strategies (see Coburn & Talbert, 2006; Militello, Sireci, & Schweid, 2008; Supovitz & Christman, 2003). (2009, p. 17)

The notion that certain types of leadership behaviors matter more than others was clarified in a meta-analysis conducted by Tim Waters and his colleagues at Mid-Continent Research for Education and Learning (McREL). Their extensive review of the literature on school leadership identified a number of key responsibilities and behaviors that, when practiced by principals, were likely to "promote significant improvement in student achievement" (Waters, Marzano, & McNulty, 2003).

HOW DO PRINCIPALS IMPACT STUDENT LEARNING?

The McREL meta-analysis identified 21 responsibilities that encompass 66 specific behaviors linked to a principal's impact on student learning. All the responsibilities and behaviors were shown to have a positive impact, but not all had the same magnitude of impact. Waters and Cameron (2007) pointed out, "Principals are asked to fulfill many and varied responsibilities that are important in running a school," but they made an important distinction when they observed that "not all of them, however, are essential to improving student achievement." (p. 18)

Waters and Cameron seemed to understand the complexity required in any effort to monitor 87 different dimensions of leadership, and they attempted to differentiate between what was *important* and what was *essential*. They explained, "Maintaining facilities, managing budgets, complying with regulations, and arranging transportation are all *important* aspects of running a school, but not *essential* to creating higher levels of student achievement" (Waters & Cameron, 2007, p. 18). What the McREL study suggested is something that many may have sensed intuitively for a long time—that not all of the responsibilities required of principals are essential to improving student achievement.

In fact, some leadership behaviors have a negative impact on student learning. Waters and Cameron wrote,

> As important as these findings are, there is another finding that is equally important. That is, just as leaders can have a positive impact on achievement, they also can have a marginal, or worse, a negative impact on achievement. When leaders concentrate on the wrong school and/or classroom practices, or miscalculate the magnitude or "order" of the change they are attempting to implement, they can negatively impact student achievement. (2007, p. 5)

To summarize, Waters and his fellow researchers at McREL discovered that the leadership a principal provides makes a difference, but some behaviors matter more when the goal is improving student learning. According to their study, some leadership behaviors are positive, and some may be negative. However, even those that are positively correlated to student learning do not all have an equal impact on student achievement.

DIFFERENT FORMS OF LEADERSHIP IMPACT LEARNING DIFFERENTLY

John Hattie extended the notion that some leadership behaviors are more important than others. In his book *Visible Learning*, Hattie (2009) separated the research into two forms of leadership—instructional leadership and transformational leadership—and found that while both had a positive impact on learning, one form of leadership was more impactful than the other.

Hattie (2012) reported on the results of a 2008 meta-analysis conducted by Robinson, Lloyd, and Rowe. In that study, the researchers found the impact on learning to have an effect size of .11 for transformational leadership and .42 for instructional leadership.

Hattie chose to use *effect size* to communicate the relative differences between various school improvement strategies reported in his work. According to Robert Coe, "Effect size is simply a way of quantifying the size of the difference between two groups. It is easy to calculate, readily understood and can be applied to any measured outcome in Education or Social Science" (2002, p. 1). Coe continues, saying, "It [effect size] is particularly valuable for quantifying the effectiveness of a particular intervention, relative to some comparison. It allows us to move beyond the simplistic, 'Does it work or not?' to the far more sophisticated, 'How well does it work in a range of contexts?'" (2002, p. 1). Hattie's choice of effect size allows educators seeking evidence of best practices to compare the relative impacts of different strategies on learning. In this case, Hattie clearly demonstrates the impact that different leadership styles have on learning, with instructional leadership being more powerful that transformational leadership.

Hattie suggests that principals are engaged in instructional leadership when they "have their major focus on creating a learning climate free of disruption, a system of clear teaching objectives, and high teacher expectations for teachers and students" (2012, p. 83). He defines transformational leadership as the behaviors principals engage in with their teaching staff in order to "inspire them to new levels of energy, commitment, and moral purpose such that they work collaboratively to overcome challenges and reach ambitious goals" (2012, p. 83). Hattie's conclusion was that when the goal is higher levels of learning for all students, the activities associated with *instructional* leadership had a greater impact than those associated with *transformational* leadership.

Robinson linked the work of Waters and Hattie when she reported that "Although Waters, Marzano, and McNulty . . . did not use the distinction between instructional and transformational leadership in their meta-analysis, the results show a similar pattern" (Hattie, 2009, p. 84). The implications for our practice are clear. As Robinson pointed out, "The more leaders focus their influence, their learning, and their relationships with teachers on the core business of teaching and learning, the greater their likely influence on student outcomes" (Robinson, 2008, p. 636).

LEADERSHIP MATTERS, BUT THE RIGHT KIND OF LEADERSHIP MATTERS MORE

A review of the literature on school leadership demonstrates that there is, in fact, "a substantial relationship between leadership and student achievement." (Waters & Cameron, 2007, p. 10). After their review of the literature, Militello, Rallis, and Goldring (2009) came to a similar conclusion. In fact, beginning as early as 1984 with John Goodlad's *A Place Called School* the importance of the principal's role in improving student achievement has never been in doubt.

We have also learned that it is not just any kind of leadership that matters. Hattie's analysis showed that some forms of leadership are more impactful than are others. He found that when the goal is improved student achievement, principals should focus on the attributes associated with an instructional leader as opposed to those of a transformational leader. The emerging view is that since some behaviors are more closely linked to higher levels of student learning than are others, principals need to be more discriminating and develop a discerning eye toward what they activities engage in during the day.

With a clear consensus emerging on the fact that a principal's leadership impacts student learning and that different types of leadership behavior impact student achievement in different ways and to different degrees, how, then, do principals focus on the strategies that matter most?

2 Examining the Complex Role of the Principal

During a typical day, principals experience thousands of interactions with hundreds of people. It is not unusual for principals to begin the day with the supervision of buses before moving on to observing classrooms, attending conferences and IEP meetings, resolving a conflict between students, attending meetings with grade-level teams, and making phone calls to parents—all before noon!

Most people would struggle with being pulled in multiple directions, but principals accomplish this on a daily basis with a calm familiarity. During those occasional moments of reflection, principals find their busy job occasionally frustrating and often inspiring but always fulfilling, because they know they are making a difference.

It is understandable, then, that when it comes to being instructional leaders, principals have a lot of factors competing for their time and attention. Their days are varied, to be sure, yet the tales they tell share some common themes. Perhaps these stories, or some version thereof, sound familiar:

- Hunched over your keyboard, you complete a multitude of tedious and required reports for the district, the state, and/or the federal government—all asking for *exactly* the same information.
- "Do you have a minute?" asks the teacher who stops by your office every day. Now, 20 minutes later, you are *so* wishing you had asked your secretary to interrupt with an "important" call from the superintendent.

- You receive an urgent summons to the boys' bathroom, where you discover mounds of unraveled toilet paper and two fourth graders pointing fingers at each other.
- Your e-mail includes daily tips from district parents guiding you to "an interesting little article I found on the Internet," each link more bizarre than the last, and each new one distracting you more than the previous one.

Every principal has stories to tell. You probably are thinking right now of some that you could offer from personal experience. Consider, for example, this story of the chaos that erupted during the lunch hour at an elementary school.

THE SHEER PANDEMONIUM OF THE PRINCIPALSHIP

As was her daily practice, the principal left her office to check on things in the cafeteria. On this day, the noise from the lunchroom seemed louder than normal, and she wondered why it seemed to be so much more than the customary chaos of lunch? She entered the cafeteria, and there, standing in front of her, was a six-foot-tall, life-sized panda, handing out candy to first and second graders! As she struggled to process what was happening, nearly 100 primary-aged students simultaneously left their seats, scrambling to surround the stranger in the panda suit and get their share of the treats!

After quickly escorting the unknown and uninvited "panda" out of the cafeteria, the principal could not even catch her breath before having more to do. First and foremost was the safety of the children, and she moved quickly to restore the lost decorum in the lunchroom. She immediately asked the nurse to check both the list of students with diabetes and the other list of those with peanut allergies. Next, she examined the treats to determine whether they qualified as a "safe snack"—yet another wellness mandate, courtesy of the board of education. While this was happening, she did her best to patiently explain to the disappointed students that no, pandas are not allowed to hand out candy at school.

All this excitement took place during a special lunch fund-raising event sponsored by the local parent organization. So even though the special lunch had been prepared by an outside vendor, the principal *still* was responsible for ensuring that (1) an approved type-A lunch was provided to all children eligible to participate in the free and reduced-price lunch program and (2) all the adults helping that day had signed in properly at the office.

The lunch hour ended with a very long talk with the well-intentioned parent who had arranged for the panda's visit, explaining why it wasn't a good idea to hire pandas—or any other animals, for that matter—without checking with the office first.

It was not as if the incident was self-contained; that would be much too easy for the already hectic day the principal had scheduled. Having spent significant time addressing the panda-monium in the cafeteria, she had to reschedule two teacher observations and miss a scheduled team meeting to review data from a recent district-level assessment.

Sound familiar? Indeed, the principal is a juggler responsible for successfully managing many complicated, diverse, and often unpredictable tasks. As the panda story illustrates, the principalship can even be occasionally chaotic. In the space of less than an hour, this principal balanced numerous managerial and supervisory responsibilities with a variety of complex policy and procedural issues while weighing the legal and regulatory repercussions of a decision she did not make.

In addition, the principal recognized and was responsive to the socio-emotional need of students, teachers, and parents and still managed to successfully meet some pretty tricky political demands. The principal in our story was exhausted and felt overwhelmed, but all the evidence suggests the principal's role is not likely to get any less complex or chaotic any time soon.

TRENDS SHAPING THE CURRENT REALITY OF THE PRINCIPALSHIP

Schools in general, and principals in particular, are responding to growing demands for improved student achievement in the face of shrinking financial resources and shifting political and professional priorities. The combination of these developments has created the perfect storm and resulted in an increasingly expanded role for principals—one that is nearing its practical capacity.

Researchers at the Center for the Future of Teaching and Learning acknowledged that instructional leadership, which they defined as "overseeing the school's core functions of teaching and learning," was the component of a principal's job most related to improved student outcomes, yet "the demands of the principalship encompass far more than just instructional leadership, and these demands are extensive and expanding" (Bland et al., 2011, p. 19). Furthermore, their research found that while studies show "the influence of the principal on student learning and achievement is second only to the classroom teacher, like their classroom counterparts, today's principals are expected to simultaneously manage a tremendous number of responsibilities" (Bland et al., 2011, p. 59).

Bland et al. cited similar findings published as part of the *Getting Down to Facts* series and pointed to "numerous studies [that] show that the time required to fulfill the management-related responsibilities is increasingly crowding out time for principals to observe, evaluate, and support teachers" (2011, p. 19). In findings similar to those of the Center for the Future of Teaching study, principals reported that "interacting with parents, interacting with district staff, and attending to discipline problems" were the activities that consumed most of their time (Fuller, Loeb, Arshan, Chen, & Yi, 2007, as reported in Bland, et al., 2011, p. 19).

These findings raise some important questions. Has the scope of the principalship pushed beyond the ability of individuals to fulfill the role? If we believe that principals have a significant impact on student learning and agree that instructional leadership is a principal's primary responsibility, then have we created conditions whereby today's principals have sufficient resources (time, money, and support) to impact teaching and learning in meaningful ways? Have the additional demands created by increasing accountability for student achievement, decreasing financial resources, and competing strategic initiatives exceeded what can reasonably be expected of principals? Several developments have contributed to the expanded role of the principalship.

Increased accountability for improved student achievement

The first development impacting principals is the push for higher levels of student achievement. This expectation began in earnest with the enactment of No Child Left Behind (NCLB). Prior to the enactment of NCLB, there were no federally mandated standards that governed accountability and testing in U.S. public schools. States (and, to a lesser extent, districts) had significant flexibility in designing their own standards for school performance monitoring and accountability. In practice, however, while most states conducted annual testing, very few had explicit consequences associated with poor performance.

Today, the reality for many principals is that their job security, compensation levels, and career advancement are increasingly tied to the results of high-stakes testing. Many factors outside a principal's control impact student achievement, and holding a principal accountable for test scores—which is different than holding principals accountable for how they *respond* to test scores—places principals in difficult, if not untenable, positions.

Decreased financial resources for people and programs

The second development impacting principals is the reduced availability of financial resources necessary to support higher levels of student achievement. School districts across the country have been cutting budgets and reducing funding levels, as economic realities and a wave of initiatives designed to limit spending have swept the nation. The result is less and less money to respond to the increasingly higher and higher demands for improving student achievement.

Education is fundamentally a "people business," with as much as 80% of the cost of schooling spent on personnel. Decreasing levels of funding typically translate into cutting support staff and administrative positions, often at the district level. When district level support staff and administrative positions are cut, the paperwork associated with state and federal programs, grants, and other legal and regulatory reporting requirements doesn't go away; it simply trickles down to the building level, adding to the scope of the principal's managerial responsibilities.

This trend of diminished funding contributes directly to the expanding role of principals who have little choice but to accept the additional managerial responsibilities. What we fail to recognize is that something has to give. These additional responsibilities often require principals to sacrifice time and attention previously spent on improving instruction.

Tighter budgets also mean fewer assistant principals, instructional coaches, clerical aides, and support staff. Reducing or eliminating these positions further impacts a principal's ability to focus on improving instruction. A California principal described how the loss of support and clerical staff affected her job: "Much of my time is 'sucked up' by dealing with peer mediation (which used to be handled by a counselor), attendance concerns (which used to be handled by a clerk), or general duties that the school secretary previously handled" (Bland et al., 2011, p. 40). As principals spend more time on managerial responsibilities, they have less time to observe teachers, monitor results, and coordinate resources to improve instruction.

The principalship has always been a balancing act between instructional and managerial responsibilities, but the balance has shifted away from instruction as management responsibilities have grown. "Today's principals have more to do, fewer people to help, and higher stakes with which to contend" (Bland et al., 2011, p. 59).

Competing strategic initiatives

A third development impacting the capacity of principals to function effectively as instructional leaders has been a flurry of new strategic initiatives that now compete for their attention. For example, the recent emphasis on implementing the Common Core State Standards and better assessment systems, coupled with the Teacher Quality Initiative and a national push for more rigorous teacher evaluation systems, have pushed aside much of the talk of 21st Century Skills and previous efforts to infuse technology into the daily routine of the classroom.

All of these initiatives are credible, all create significant opportunities for principals, and all are worthy of careful consideration. However, while all of these are important initiatives, they can't all be the *most* important initiative. If everything is important, then nothing is important! The adoption of any one of these initiatives would require a significant commitment of time, energy, and resources by principals. The lack of clarity around what matters most makes it virtually impossible for principals to focus their limited resources on a single, worthwhile initiative.

The lack of priorities is not limited to national initiatives. When superintendents or boards of education constantly change direction, principals find themselves navigating through the turbulence created by shifting priorities at the local level. For principals, these local initiatives often take on the characteristics of organizational "fire drills" in that they are urgent, unrelated to teaching and learning, and someone else's priority.

Schmoker writes, "Priority is a function of simplicity, and it dictates that we only focus on a few things at a time—namely, on those elements that are most likely to help us achieve our goals" (2011, p. 14). A lack of priorities—or priorities that are constantly changing as evidenced by ever-changing lists of plans, projects, and proposals, all of which seem to take precedence over the previous one—slows organizational momentum and undermines commitment.

Knowing the right thing to do is the central problem of school improvement.

—(Elmore, 2003, p. 9)

In her study of the principalship, Linda Darling-Hammond documented the growing responsibilities of the principal's role. She reported, "The role of principal has swelled to include a staggering array of professional tasks and competencies. Principals are expected to be educational visionaries, instructional and curriculum leaders, assessment experts, disciplinarians, community builders, public information and communication experts, budget analysts, facility managers, special program administrators, as well as guardians of various legal, contractual, and policy mandates and initiatives" (Darling-Hammond & Bransford, 2005, p. 3).

These developments are converging and suggest the need to refine our perception of the principalship. First, the literature has established that an effective principal is critical to successful schools. Second, a growing body of evidence has confirmed that the principal's job is both complex and challenging. Finally, there is consensus on which organizational practices improve student achievement (these are discussed in Chapter 3), but while the research is pointing us toward specific strategies that promote student learning, the reality is that identifying the highest priorities remains a vexing problem for most principals.

We know a lot about the principal's impact on student learning, but what we do not know is how to help principals identify, implement, and sustain the specific strategies that make a difference in student achievement. According to Darling-Hammond, "While there is increasing research on how principals influence school effectiveness, less is known about how to help principals develop the capacities that make a difference in how schools function and what students learn" (2005, p. 4).

Becoming an instructional leader is an aspiration worthy of one's best effort, but the role of "instructional leader" may not be as deeply embedded in the principalship as expected. In 2009, Turnbull et al. found the typical perception was that principals spent 70% of their time on instruction and 30% on managerial tasks, but a carefully designed time study reported that principals actually spent 70% of their time on management responsibilities and only 30% on tasks related to their role as instructional leaders.

Add to this reality the fact that a principal's professional isolation may be even greater than that of teachers, and it becomes obvious that most principals have too few opportunities to share, reflect, and build a deeper level of understanding of how to respond to the demanding nature of their jobs. It is clear that what would help principals most would be a way to help them identify a few high-leverage strategies that were likely to have the greatest impact on student achievement.

CREATING A NEW NORMAL FOR PRINCIPALS

Earlier we tried to describe a normal day for a principal, but the phrase "normal day" may represent an oxymoron for most principals. No two days are alike, and it doesn't appear that we will be able to create a new "normal" for principals anytime soon. Being a principal is often complicated, challenging, and complex, yet many very effective principals still find ways to ensure that all children learn. How do they do it?

3 Move the World

The Essence of Leverage

Give me a lever long enough and I could move the world.

—Archimedes

In their study of the principalship, the Wallace Foundation observed, "Although the vast majority of participating principals wanted to be instructional leaders, few could articulate a vision of what an instructional leader does or which activities would be the highest priorities" (Turnbull et al., 2009, p. 2). Their researchers concluded that principals need help in identifying the strategies that would produce the greatest results in their schools.

In summarizing their findings, Jody Spiro suggested the next logical direction for researchers was to "identify the high-leverage strategies that will get the 'biggest bang for the buck' in instruction" (Turnbull et al., 2009, p. 2). The Wallace Foundation was not alone in suggesting that helping principals identify high-leverage strategies was an area of need.

Given that time in school is precious, *especially for principals*, it makes sense to identify the strategies that have the most leverage. But, if collating and publishing lists is all we do, principals are left with the same dilemma: "Of all these strategies, which one do we begin with?" We have yet to adequately address the need to help principals identify the high-leverage strategies that will improve their schools.

It is hard to disagree with the principle of leverage.

—Senge, 1990, p. 114

Leverage is defined as the least amount of energy needed to generate the greatest amount of improvement. When building leaders use the principles of leverage to identify the best strategies to improve their schools, they engage in a two-step process. First, they ask themselves if the strategy is likely to be successful—is it effective? Second, they ask themselves if the strategy is doable—is it viable? It makes no sense to invest in strategies that are not likely to be successful, nor is it logical to commit to a strategy that sounds good on paper but does not work in practice. For a strategy to be considered high leverage, it must be both effective and viable.

The first question associated with the principles of leverage focuses on effectiveness: Will this strategy generate the desired outcome? Involving others in the investigation of the effectiveness of a strategy builds shared knowledge and generates commitment among the faculty and staff. The rationale for engaging staff in the school improvement process is simple; the more the faculty is involved, the more positively they will respond. However, involvement can be a time-consuming task, and the sense of urgency for principals to rapidly move schools in a positive direction has never been more palpable. Torben Rick argues that the pressure to act undermines engagement as "leaders take drastic steps quickly with no time to explore alternatives" (2012, p. 1). He suggests that deeply held "values about participation, involvement, or concern for people can disappear" (Rick, 2012, p. 1) under the pressure for immediate results. To answer this initial question of leverage, it is best to work with others and seek out all the available research and evidence to determine if the strategy will likely result in higher levels of learning for students.

At the same time, it is essential principals acknowledge that not all strategies are equally effective. In *Visible Learning*, John Hattie (2012) reported that nearly every educational innovation has some level of support in the literature. He wrote, "When teachers claim that they are having a positive effect on achievement or when a policy improves achievement, this is almost a trivial claim, because virtually everything works. In fact, one only needs a pulse to improve achievement" (Hattie, 2012, p. 15). He also cautioned educators that the magnitude of the impact a strategy has on student learning can vary wildly from one strategy to the next. A few examples illustrate the fact that not all strategies are equally effective.

To no one's surprise, Hattie reported that small class size had a positive impact on learning; the effect size (Coe, 2002) for class size was .21, which ranked it 113th on the list of 150 factors he studied. Looking at class size through the lens of leverage, a principal's thinking might go something like this: "Does small class size have a positive impact on student learning? Yes, but how does the impact of class size compare to the impact of other strategies?" The impact of small class size is dwarfed by the impact of several other strategies such as formative feedback (an effect size of .90 and rank of 4th), teacher clarity (an effect size of .75 and a rank of 9th), and the provision of high-quality feedback (an effect size of .73 and a rank of 10th). Obviously class size matters, but if principals are deciding what strategies to pursue to improve student learning, they have to acknowledge that class size is not nearly as impactful as some other strategies.

Another example further illustrates why it is important that principals understand not all strategies are equally impactful. Teaching students test-taking skills is a strategy that has a marginal impact on student learning, yet a lot of time and energy has gone into developing programs that prepare students to take the high-stakes, end-of-year tests. A principal might ask, "Does student achievement really benefit from understanding test-taking strategies? Are there other strategies that might have a greater impact?" Hattie (2009) found the positive impact of teaching test-taking skills (an effect size of .27 and a rank of 98th) could not compare with the impact of teaching study skills (an effect size of .63 and a rank of 22nd). In terms of leverage, teaching study skills was nearly three times as impactful as teaching test-taking skills.

To reiterate, building principals must choose their school improvement strategies on the basis of effectiveness, all the while acknowledging that not every strategy is equally effective when it comes to promoting higher levels of learning. This is an important insight, because, as Hattie's (2009) research illustrates, there are many tactics, strategies, and approaches that are positive but each has varying degrees of impact on school improvement.

The second question principals consider when choosing a strategy is whether or not a strategy is viable. A strategy cannot be high leverage unless it is effective, but just because a strategy is effective does not make it high leverage. It must also be viable. To paraphrase James Popham (2008), things that are more sophisticated or complicated are often regarded as preferable to things that are unsophisticated and uncomplicated, but with respect to learning, this is not always the case.

When examining this second dimension of leverage, principals seek out examples or find similar settings where a school or faculty has been able to successfully implement the strategy. The question of viability addresses the practicality of an idea; is it "doable"? No matter how effective a strategy might be, if it is too complex, too expensive, or too time and personnel intensive to implement successfully, then the strategy has no leverage.

Mike Mattos captured the spirit of the viable dimension of a high-leverage strategy when he wrote,

> Too many times 'purists' recommend 'research-based' practices that are virtually impossible to implement in real-life classrooms, while questioning practitioners that are getting proven results with practices that do not strictly adhere to their rigid research proto-cols. . . . I find it surprising that critics seem to place absolute faith in results obtained through the study of a limited number of schools in a controlled setting, while dismissing results that are being consistently replicated by hundreds of real-life schools, of varying sizes and demographics. (personal communication, September 3, 2011)

Mattos properly places high value on the applicability of strategies—their viability—and makes a good case for the notion that if a strategy cannot be replicated across a significant number of classrooms, the strategy is not a high-leverage strategy.

Bob Marzano provides an excellent example of a high-leverage strategy—one that is both effective and viable—when he encourages teachers to have students track their own progress using graphic displays. This practice provides two important kinds of information for students and staff: clear expectation for learning, and feedback on a student's progress toward the learning target. The strategy is simple yet powerful. According to Marzano, the practice of having students track their own progress was associated with a 32 percentile point gain in their achievement (Marzano, 2009). Classrooms at all levels can use this strategy to enhance student achievement. Some teachers create classroom data displays that students update on a regular basis, while others have students track their own progress on charts kept in individual folders. Typically a presentation during a faculty meeting coupled with some follow-up from a coach or a team leader is sufficient to implement the idea.

On the other hand, Doug Reeves (2002) provides an example of a low-leverage strategy—one that is both ineffective and not viable—when he describes the impact strategic planning has on improving schools. The strategic planning process produces a plan of action, but far too often the plan itself becomes the end rather than a means to an end. In those unfortunate cases, school districts have invested tremendous resources, and the only result is a bookshelf filled with color-coordinated binders. The strategic planning process takes a tremendous commitment of time, money, and personnel by an entire organization yet, according to Reeves, produces almost no measurable impact on student learning.

CREATING AN OPERATIONAL DEFINITION OF LEVERAGE

Results-oriented leaders focus on the few things that are most influential in achieving their most important goals.

—Sparks, 2005, p. 25

By using high-leverage strategies—those that are both effective and viable—principals can impact their schools in ways that can be significant and sustained. Our working definition requires a strategy to be both effective *and* viable to be considered high leverage. Table 3.1 illustrates the way these two dimensions interact.

Table 3.1   Leverage Matrix

	Less Viable	More Viable
More Effective	**Quadrant 3** More Effective Less Viable	**Quadrant 4** More Effective More Viable
Less Effective	**Quadrant 1** Less Effective Less Viable	**Quadrant 2** Less Effective More Viable

1. Strategies in Quadrant 1 have the least leverage. Strategies in this quadrant have some support in the literature or popular culture, but they are neither effective nor viable enough to substantially improve teaching and learning. This quadrant reflects the least effective and least viable approaches for principals.

2. Strategies in Quadrant 2 have some leverage and are more viable but are no more effective than a Quadrant 1 strategy. A strategy in this quadrant may be easy to implement but is relatively inconsequential in terms of its impact on teaching and learning.

3. Strategies in Quadrant 3 may also have some leverage and are characterized as more effective but are no more viable than a Quadrant 1 strategy. A strategy in this quadrant may promote higher levels of learning but is somewhat difficult to implement, which reduces its impact on teaching and learning.

4. Strategies in Quadrant 4 have the most leverage. A strategy in Quadrant 4 has significant support in the literature or popular culture and is both effective and viable enough to impact teaching and learning. This quadrant reflects the most effective and most viable approaches for principals.

WHERE CAN WE LOOK FOR THE LEVERAGE POINT?

There are no simple rules for finding high-leverage changes, but there are ways of thinking that make it more likely.

—Senge, 1990, p. 65

Before we illustrate the dimensions of leverage by analyzing the choices of four principals who set similar goals for their schools, we need to add the notion of leverage points to our understanding of leverage. Leverage points are the purposeful actions or changes principals make in the structures (policies, practices, and procedures) of their schools that result in higher levels of learning for students. A leverage point is an actionable, conscious, and intentional decision within the purview of, achievable by, and chosen by the building principal.

A metaphor for leverage points was offered by Peter Senge when citing Buckminster Fuller's concept of a trim tab—a small rudder on the rudder of a ship. According to Senge, the trim tab's function it is "to make it easier to turn the rudder, which, then, makes it easier to turn the ship" (Senge, 1990, p. 64).

Donella Meadows encourages leaders to make intentional use the principles of leverage by looking for leverage points, which she defines as "places [or pressure points] within a complex system where a small shift in one thing can produce big changes in everything" (Meadows, n.d., para. 1). She provided an example of leverage points when she described the impact that having easy access to timely and accurate information had on energy consumption.

Meadows reported on a project to reduce energy consumption in a subdivision of nearly identical suburban houses. In some homes, the electric meter was installed in the basement. In others, it was installed in the front hall where the homeowner could conveniently and routinely see the dial.

When there were no other differences to account for, electricity consumption was 30% lower in the houses where the meter was in the front hall. In this example, easy access to timely and accurate information was the high-leverage strategy. The location of the meter was the leverage point.

There are many places principals can look for leverage points, but Senge suggests a good place to begin looking is within an organization's structures.

The challenge for leaders is seeing where actions and small changes in structures can lead to significant, enduring improvements.

—Senge, 1990, p. 114

Sometimes leverage points are not within the individual strategies themselves, but in the way several strategies are assembled or integrated together. Other times, a leverage point is found by emphasizing organizational priorities through applying a fresh approach to an old structure. At times a leverage point is found in the data and measurement of specific outcomes. Almost always, leverage increases as the conversation moves toward people's values, attitudes, and beliefs.

Recognizing which of those seemingly insignificant actions will have a profoundly positive impact on a school is the leader's challenge. To illustrate the process of identifying leverage points in your school, consider the following leverage points principals chose to promote higher levels of learning for their students.

Create a master schedule that reflects the priorities of high-leverage strategies

The way principals assemble and integrate priorities into the school's master schedule represents a powerful leverage point. Whenever we visit schools, we ask to see a copy of the master schedule and look for two things. First, we see if there is evidence that at least one hour a week is set aside for teachers to meet during the regular school day. This designated and protected team time promotes development of a collaborative culture. Second, we verify that opportunities exist for students to access more time and support without missing direct instruction in the core subject areas. Schedules that reflect this second priority support the development of schoolwide and systematic pyramids of intervention.

Changing a master schedule to reflect time for both collaboration and intervention is an example of a leverage point. The principal's increased leverage comes from the integration of priorities to ensure the school's policies, practices, and procedures align with the high-leverage strategies of collaboration and interventions. Because teams are given time to meet, they are better able to identify struggling students by name and need. When leveraged together, these two ideas make for a powerful combination.

Change the focus of traditional faculty meetings

Principals can find a readily available leverage point by simply shifting the tone and tenor of traditional faculty meetings from logistics to learning. Instead of sharing verbal memos, the most effective principals consciously choose to use faculty meetings for professional learning. Minimizing time spent reviewing procedural issues in order to maximize time spent sharing best practices is an example of a small change (but a powerful leverage point) that reinforces learning as the fundamental purpose of the school.

Repurposing faculty meetings is an example of how principals find leverage by using a fresh approach to an old structure. In this example, changing the focus of the traditional faculty meeting is a leverage point that can create priceless opportunities for additional training and job-embedded staff development.

Create a schoolwide schedule for common assessments

Using results of common formative assessments to guide instruction is another high-leverage strategy. Principals find that leverage comes from measurement—the identification of which students were successful and which strategies were most effective—which allows teams to use data to drive instruction.

The simple act of publishing an assessment schedule (the leverage point in this example) that targets when teams will be expected to administer common assessments is a purposeful action that ensures formative data will be available to teams. Publishing and monitoring an assessment schedule are leverage points within every principal's sphere of influence.

Create meaningful collaborative teams

Another powerful high-leverage strategy is realized by simply requiring every teacher—including special education teachers—to be members of meaningful collaborative teams. Research has shown that making the small change of including special education teachers on regular education teams improves the pedagogy of *both* regular and special education teachers.

Regular education teachers realize the instructional strategies designed to help students with disabilities also help students without disabilities. Likewise, as special education teachers participate in discussions and professional development activities designed to improve instruction for students without disabilities, their practice improves. Insisting that all teachers work together in this new teaming structure dissolves the false dichotomy between regular and special education teachers and provides an opportunity for teachers to examine their beliefs around the idea that *all* kids can learn.

Leverage points represent powerful points of change for principals. For each initiative there is typically an opportunity for a small change or adjustment (a leverage point) that makes it more likely a particular high-leverage strategy will be successful.

How do the principles of leverage and leverage points impact teaching and learning in our schools? The following scenarios demonstrate how leaders have attempted to use the principles of leverage to improve their schools by focusing on activities that had more or less leverage. Not all the strategies are equally effective or viable, and as the scenarios illustrate, each principal could have improved the results by looking for leverage points in each of the chosen strategies.

Quadrant 1 Strategies

Collecting individual teachers' lesson plans is an example of a practice that is neither effective nor viable.

In the first school, the principal set a goal to improve teaching and learning by monitoring the planning process of teachers. Based on the belief that more effective planning will lead to more effective lessons and ultimately produce higher levels of student achievement, this principal chose to collect and review individual teachers' lesson plans on a weekly basis. The hope was that if the principal inspected individual lesson plans on a regular basis, teachers would do a better job of aligning their instruction to the agreed-upon standards. The reality was that, while inspecting individual lesson plans allowed the principal to monitor the planning and preparation of individual teachers, it proved a time-consuming task that had a minimal impact on learning.

The principal could accomplish the same goal of monitoring planning by shifting the focus from collecting individual lesson plans and evaluating them in isolation to holding meetings with teams of teachers to review the upcoming unit plans before instruction begins. A collective conversation about unit plans with teachers is a better way to meet the goal of monitoring the planning process for several reasons.

First and foremost, it allows teachers to take advantage of the shared expertise of the team. It also allows the principal to ask some very important questions about the alignment between what teachers are planning to teach and the guaranteed and viable curriculum, the match between the learning target and the learning task, how students will be assessed, and what plans are in place to support students who have or have not learned what was expected.

Quadrant 2 Strategies

Using classroom walkthrough protocols is an example of a practice that can be efficient but is not viable.

In the second school, the principal set the same goal of improving instruction but chose one of the many variations of classroom walkthrough protocols as the strategy to achieve the goal. As implemented in this school, classroom walkthroughs represented a low-leverage strategy.

This principal committed to walk the building and look for evidence of specific teaching behaviors. The principal self-selected the behaviors without consulting with teachers but was confident they were appropriate, because the "look-fors" were based upon a list of highly effective teaching practices compiled by the district office and reflective of the state's new teacher evaluation system. Furthermore, it was decided not to burden teachers with any feedback, since the protocol was primarily designed to help sharpen the principal's observation skills.

Classroom walkthroughs become little more than a break from the office routine unless they are well implemented. The principal completed the walkthroughs whenever possible, but from time to time, the press of daily routines caused the principal to reschedule the visits or conduct the walkthroughs by engaging in RWWOTD (reflecting while walking out the door) at the end of the day. Even though the principal was able to gather mountains of observational data in an expeditious manner, little was shared with teachers and thus the classroom walkthroughs had a minimal impact on learning.

A more effective and viable strategy to accomplish the same goal is to cultivate the habit of conducting quick drop-in visits of three to five classrooms every day to look for evidence of teaching behaviors linked to school goals. Within 24 hours of the visit, the principal follows up with a face-to-face conversation with the teacher to share what was observed.

In this case, a shift from the use of a formal walkthrough protocol based on external criteria to a more authentic approach grounded in a valid, school-based problem of practice has several advantages. First, focusing on goals identified by the teachers themselves will ultimately generate far more ownership than using criteria identified by external consultants or district-level personnel. Next, scheduling of the strategy is more flexible, since the visits are short, impromptu visits unrelated to the formal teacher evaluation process. Finally, the credibility of the strategy is higher, since the teaching behaviors the principal is looking for are linked to school goals teachers helped identify, design, and adopt. This strategy also creates a stronger Results Orientation by building in a feedback loop and celebrating the teaching behaviors the principal wants to see repeated

Quadrant 3 Strategies

Teaching a model lesson in an individual classroom is an example of a practice that can be effective but not viable.

In the third school, the principal set a similar goal of improving instruction but chose to teach a series of model lessons linked to the teacher evaluation process. The goal was to support classroom teachers and improve instruction by differentiating the level of support using model lessons to demonstrate effective teaching practices. While this approach may have been effective, it was not viable.

As an extension of the formal teacher evaluation process, teachers identified an area of growth they wanted to learn more about. Next, the principal planned and delivered a demonstration lesson using methodology aligned with the growth target, while the teacher observed and took notes. The teacher and the principal later met to discuss the model lesson and collaboratively plan the next lesson. The process continued as the teacher redelivered their own lesson using the new methodology, while the principal observed and took notes. Finally, the process ended when the teacher and principal met to discuss new insights the teacher had gained from the process. This cycle was repeated over and over throughout the school year, as individual teachers chose methodologies based on growth targets identified during the teacher evaluation process.

Modeling lessons that demonstrate effective teaching practices is an effective way to change behavior; the literature is full of research- and evidence-based support for this strategy. In total, the principal likely spent five to six hours preparing, planning, delivering, and debriefing the model lesson. If this is done well, the principal has a positive impact on a single teacher and a single classroom of students. However, those same five or six hours were most likely taken from time that might have been used with another teacher who also needed help in improving practice and pedagogy. As this strategy was implemented, this principal used an approach that was helpful but so time intensive that it was not sustainable. The principal could have chosen a different approach—one that maintained the overall effectiveness of the approached but increased the viability—by using a lesson study protocol to accomplish the same goal.

In lesson study, a team of teachers chooses a common growth target and designs a model lesson together. The teachers observe one another as the lesson is taught, meet to deconstruct and redesign the lesson based on observational data, and observe each other again as the redesigned lesson is redelivered. If this principal attended the meetings of the team involved in the lesson study and devoted approximately the same five or six hours to helping teachers improve their instructional practices, the principal would impact an entire team of teachers and several classrooms of students. During the course of working with the team, this principal could have modeled collaboration and using data to drive instruction, reinforced effective teaching practices, and leveraged the same amount of time to impact four times as many teachers and students.

Quadrant 4 Strategies

Using common assessment data to drive instructional decision making is an example of a practice that can be both effective and viable.

In the fourth school, the principal set the same goal of improving instruction but chose to focus on the ways teachers used assessment data. The strategy chosen was to improve instruction by using the results of common, formative assessments to drive instructional decision making. This approach to school improvement was both effective and viable.

For several years, teachers had analyzed data from quarterly benchmark assessments to identify areas of the curriculum where students were not proficient. During districtwide "data days," teams of teachers received prepackaged folders filled with tables, graphs, and reports prepared by the assessment department. The data were organized by school, department, and/or grade level, but results for individual classrooms were not returned to teachers. After a requisite presentation by district administrators, teachers were given an opportunity to look at the various reports with colleagues.

The principal decided to shift the focus of how data were used by advocating for the use of more frequent and formative assessments developed collaboratively at the school site. Teams worked to identify the most important things students should learn, explored how to write valid and reliable assessments using high-quality test items, and trained on the use of protocols to enhance collaboration and data analysis. Each team wrote, administered, and analyzed results of a common assessment before evaluating the strategy of short-cycle assessment at a faculty meeting.

The result of this effort to improve classroom instruction through better use of data was a success. Teachers reported that they felt every time the team members met to look at data, they sharpened their pedagogy and deepened their content knowledge. They also shared the belief that working together gave them a better sense of where all the students in the grade level were and how to help the students achieve even more.

Tackling a difficult problem is often a matter of seeing where the high leverage lies.

—Sparks, 2005, p. 64

These four scenarios all took place in schools. All the principals had the same or similar goals, and all chose to use specific strategies that enjoyed research- or evidence-based support in the literature to achieve their goals. Even though each strategy was designed to improve teaching and learning, some clearly had more leverage than others.

As we argue in Chapter 4, what matters most in school improvement is best captured by the big ideas of a Professional Learning Community (PLC). We believe there are specific strategies successful principals can leverage to ensure the big ideas of a PLC take root and flourish in their schools.

These high-leverage strategies consist of complex—but not *complicated*—ideas that promote high levels of learning for all. These strategies are research or evidence based and can be replicated, targeted, limited in scope, and focused on a school's greatest area of need.

High-leverage strategies align with all of the three big ideas of a PLC. Most important of all, high-leverage strategies are practices that promote high levels of learning for all. In the next chapter we examine why we believe the use of PLCs is *the* high-leverage strategy for improving schools.

4 Professional Learning Communities

The High-Leverage Strategy

Professional learning communities have emerged as arguably the best, most agreed-upon means to improve instruction and student performance.

—Schmoker (2006, p. 106)

Since the 1990s, the Professional Learning Communities (PLCs) model has garnered support from some of the most thoughtful and influential thinkers of our times. Prominent researchers, scholars, and authors have identified the powerful and positive effects of organizing schools around the principles of PLCs. Reform-focused foundations, educational organizations, and labor unions have promoted the model as a way to improve schools. And most important, practitioners in classrooms across North America have embraced PLCs as the best way to ensure high levels of learning for all.

In an address to the National Staff Development Council in 1995, Milbrey McLaughlin said, "The most promising strategy for sustained, substantive school improvement is building the capacity of school personnel to function as a professional learning community. The path to change in the classroom lies within and through professional learning communities." McLaughlin has been joined by other prominent researchers such as Barth, Byrk, Darling-Hammond, Hord, Elmore, Warren-Little, Sergiovanni, and Hattie, all of whom have recognized PLCs as one of the best way to improve our schools.

For more than 20 years, Rick and Becky DuFour and Bob Eaker have led a group of prominent authors and practitioners that includes the likes of Fullan, Hargreaves, Marzano, Reeves, Saphier, Schmoker, and Stiggins who have also encouraged educators to embrace the PLC model. Their comments echo those of Dennis Sparks, who wrote, "Well-implemented professional learning communities are a powerful means of seamlessly blending teaching and professional learning in ways that produce complex, intelligent behavior in all teachers" (2005, p. 156).

During this same period, nearly every significant educational organization, professional association, and institution has identified PLCs as the most effective way to improve our schools. In 2004, the Annenberg Institute offered its endorsement and wrote,

> We support and encourage the use of professional learning communities (PLCs) as a central element for effective professional development and a comprehensive reform initiative. In our experience, PLCs have the potential to enhance the professional culture within a school district. (2004, p. 3)

PLCs have enjoyed the support of organizations such as the NEA, AFT, NAESP, NASSP, and Learning Forward (formerly NSDC); all have advocated for PLCs as the vehicle for improving schools.

Andy Hargreaves declared, "Professional Learning Communities (PLCs) are no longer unusual or controversial." Hargreaves continued, "Professional learning communities will soon be as accepted a part of school life as notebooks, performance evaluations and good old-fashioned chalk" (Hargreaves & Fink, 2004, p. 175). The depth and breadth of support for PLCs has never been more comprehensive, more consistent, or more coherent. It is clear that the PLC model is *the* high-leverage strategy for improving schools.

Such widespread support for PLCs has not been lost on those working to improve our schools. Perhaps Newmann and Wehlage spoke to principals best when they wrote, "If schools [principals] want to enhance their organizational capacity to boost student learning, they should work on building a professional learning community" (1995, p. 37).

AN OVERVIEW OF THE PLC MODEL

Schools working to become PLCs are clear about what is important. Principals in these schools embrace the essence of a PLC as articulated within the three big ideas of a Focus on Learning, Collaborative Culture, and Results Orientation. A clear definition of each of the three big ideas helps principals concentrate on what is important in their schools.

Big idea 1: A Focus on Learning

When a faculty embraces a Focus on Learning, teachers commit to learning as the fundamental purpose of their school. In these schools, teams of teachers work to (1) clarify the knowledge, skills, and dispositions all students must acquire; (2) monitor each student's learning on a timely basis; (3) provide systematic, timely, and directive interventions when students don't learn; and (4) develop strategies to enrich and extend the learning for students who are proficient.

Principals in these schools work tirelessly to establish the necessary conditions to foster a vibrant Focus on Learning. Reaching agreement on what all students should know and be able to do is an ongoing process and a legitimate use of teachers' time. Principals in successful schools establish the proper structures while simultaneously engaging teachers in reflective collaboration to answer to the critical questions of learning.

While teachers work to reach consensus on what students should learn, principals focus their attention on creating systems that ensure teachers have timely access to accurate data regarding student mastery of the agreed-upon standards. This is important, because, as Sam Redding observed, "Assessment provides an operational definition of standards in that it defines in measurable terms what teachers should teach and students should learn" (2006, p. 86). In schools functioning as PLCs, principals insist teachers use assessment results to determine if students are learning.

Finally, principals make sure teachers use the feedback from their assessments to provide students with additional time and support. Principals recognize the importance of creating "a systematic process of interventions to ensure students receive additional time and support for learning when they experience difficulty" (DuFour, DuFour, Eaker, & Many, 2006, p. 3). Together with their faculties, principals search for answers to these critical questions of learning.

Big idea 2: A Collaborative Culture

In schools with Collaborative Cultures, principals recognize that the foundation of a PLC is the high-performing collaborative team. Every teacher is part of a team "in which members work together interdependently to achieve a common goal for which they are mutually accountable" (DuFour et al., 2006, p. 26).

Principals promote collaboration by embracing a concept described in the literature as *directed autonomy.* According to Rick DuFour, principals who promote a culture of directed autonomy "encourage teacher autonomy and creativity (loose) within a systematic framework that stipulates clear, non-discretionary priorities and parameters (tight)" (2007, p. 49). A culture of directed autonomy is at the heart of the kind of highly effective, self-directed, interdependent collaborative teams present in successful PLCs.

In the most effective schools, principals create schedules that provide designated and protected time for teacher collaboration during the regular school day. Etienne Wenger (1998) proposed that when learning in communities of practice, participants gradually absorb and are absorbed in a "culture of practice," giving them exemplars and leading to shared meanings, a sense of belonging and increased understanding.

PLCs are distinguished by their emphasis on collective learning. King and Newmann highlight the link between the individual and collective learning, saying

> To be sure, high quality instruction depends upon the competence and attitudes of each individual teacher. But in addition, teachers' individual knowledge, skills and dispositions must be put to use in an organized, collective enterprise. That is, social resources must be cultivated, and the desired vision for social resources within a school can be summarized as professional community. (2001, p. 89)

Together, these teachers establish team norms, draft SMART (strategic and specific, measurable, attainable, results-oriented, and time-bound) goals, and identify protocols to promote more productive working relationships. They work collaboratively to clarify essential outcomes and establish clear learning targets by class, course, and grade level; cooperatively develop common assessments and analyze assessment results; and collectively plan for interventions and instructional improvement strategies.

As McLaughlin and Talbert observed, teacher collaboration in strong professional learning communities "improve the quality and equity of student learning," promotes discussions that are grounded in evidence and analysis rather than opinion, and fosters collective responsibility for student success. (2006, p. 12).

Big idea 3: A Results Orientation

Schools with a healthy Results Orientation constantly seek out evidence that students are learning at high levels. In these schools, principals encourage and support faculty members in the efficient and effective use of data in a continuous improvement process, a process solely devoted to provide timely and accurate information about student learning to teachers, teacher teams, and the school. Teachers in schools with a robust Results Orientation embrace the belief that their policies, practices, and procedures can and do promote high levels of learning for all students.

REFLECTION PROMOTES PROGRESS TOWARD BECOMING A PLC: A CASE STUDY

It is difficult to see how a PLC could develop in a school without active support at all levels of the school system. As demonstrated in Allen Parish, Louisiana, the evidence suggests that the success of any educational reform depends on the link between the individual and collective capacity of educators to function as a PLC and the system's capacity to promote student learning.

Schools in Allen Parish were filled with dedicated, passionate teachers and principals who shared a belief that all students can learn to high levels. Educators in the system had been working to establish PLCs in their schools for two years. But, like so many schools across the country, they struggled with rigorous state accountability systems and mounting federal mandates.

The widely held belief was that children in Allen Parish schools were making progress. School leaders found significant support for the theoretical underpinnings of PLCs, but roadblocks had surfaced around the practical implementation. In many schools, structures were mislabeled and definitions were confusing. Practical examples of the three big ideas were missing or underdeveloped. Building principals reported a need for help in understanding the key concepts, structures, and vocabulary of PLCs. Others struggled with the day-to-day operation of PLCs in their schools.

Mindful of the urgency to improve, parish leaders sought to identify the current reality around their PLC implementation. Principals and teachers looked for data and tangible evidence of progress that would help identify what next steps to take, but nothing was readily available. The decision was made to conduct a reflective audit of their practices in an effort to answer some of their questions.

A reflective audit involves the faculty and staff in thoughtful reflection on important structural and cultural elements of a PLC. Teachers and principals began the process by responding to a survey to assess their knowledge of PLC concepts (see Figure 4.1). The survey was followed by on-site visits and interviews focused on a school's culture, attitudes, and beliefs. Each school submitted a portfolio of school improvement plans and student achievement results. These artifacts were used to identify the presence of such important components as team norms, protocols, and SMART goals. Examples of an agreed-upon set of essential outcomes,

Figure 4.1 PLC Elements Greatest Area of Need Survey

Below is a list of elements that are essential to developing a Professional Learning Community. Individually, silently, and *honestly* assess the current reality of your school's implementation of each indicator listed in the left hand column. Consider what evidence or anecdotes support your assessment. (This form may also be used to assess district or team implementation.) Follow the directions at the top of columns two and three to begin using this tool as a self-assessment to help determine the Greatest Area of Need (GAN) for your school.

Elements of a Professional Learning Community	Indicators of a Professional Learning Community	Rate **A** = N/A; doesn't fit **B** = We need to work on this! **C** = Partially in place, occasional **D** = In place, frequently observed **Circle your ratings**				Prioritize Of those rated **B** (partially in place) or **C** (need to work on), rate the priority level for each one. **1** = High priority **2** = Medium priority **3** = Low priority **Circle your rankings**		
1. We have a clear sense of our collective purpose, the school we are attempting to create to achieve that purpose, the commitments we must make and honor to become that school, and the specific goals that will help monitor our progress.	1. It is evident that learning for all is our core purpose.	A	B	C	D	1	2	3
	2. We have a shared understanding of and commitment to the school we are attempting to create.	A	B	C	D	1	2	3
	3. We have made commitments to each other regarding how we must behave in order to achieve our mission.	A	B	C	D	1	2	3
	4. We have articulated our long-term priorities, short-term targets, and timelines for achieving those targets.	A	B	C	D	1	2	3

(Continued)

Figure 4.1 (Continued)

Elements of a Professional Learning Community	Indicators of a Professional Learning Community	Rate **A** = N/A; doesn't fit **B** = We need to work on this! **C** = Partially in place, occasional **D** = In place, frequently observed Circle your ratings	Prioritize Of those rated **B** (partially in place) or **C** (need to work on), rate the priority level for each one. **1** = High priority **2** = Medium priority **3** = Low priority Circle your rankings
2. We understand the purpose and priorities of our school because they have been communicated consistently and effectively.	5. The school has established a clear purpose and priorities that have been effectively communicated. Systems are in place to ensure action steps aligned with the purpose and priorities are implemented and aligned.	A B C D	1 2 3
	6. The leaders in the school communicate purpose and priorities through modeling, allocation of resources, what they celebrate, and what they are willing to confront.	A B C D	1 2 3
3. We acknowledge that the fundamental purpose of our school is to help all students achieve high levels of learning, and therefore, we work collaboratively to clarify what students must learn and how we will monitor each student's learning.	7. We work with our colleagues on our team to build shared knowledge regarding state, provincial, and/or national standards; district curriculum guides; trends in student achievement; and expectations for the next course or grade level. This collective inquiry has enabled each member of our team to clarify what all students must know and be able to do as a result of every unit of instruction.	A B C D	1 2 3

	8. We work with colleagues on our team to clarify the criteria by which we will judge the quality of student work, and practice applying those criteria until we can do so consistently.	A B C D	1 2 3
	9. We monitor the progress of each student's attainment of all essential outcomes on a timely basis through a series of frequent, team-developed common formative assessments that are aligned with high stakes assessments students will be required to take.	A B C D	1 2 3
4. We acknowledge that the fundamental purpose of our school is to help all students achieve high levels of learning, and therefore, we provide students with systematic interventions when they struggle and enrichment when they are proficient. (Page 106)	10. We provide a system of interventions that guarantees each student will receive additional time and support for learning if he or she experiences initial difficulty.	A B C D	1 2 3
	11. Students who are proficient have access to enriched and extended learning opportunities.	A B C D	1 2 3
5. We are committed to working together to achieve our collective purpose of learning for all students. We cultivate a collaborative culture through the development of high performing teams.	12. We are organized into collaborative teams in which members work interdependently to achieve common goals that directly impact student achievement. Structures have been put into place to ensure: a. Collaboration is embedded in our routine work practices, b. We are provided with time to collaborate,		

(Continued)

Figure 4.1 (Continued)

Elements of a Professional Learning Community	Indicators of a Professional Learning Community	Rate **A** = N/A; doesn't fit **B** = We need to work on this! **C** = Partially in place, occasional **D** = In place, frequently observed Circle your ratings	Prioritize Of those rated **B** (partially in place) or **C** (need to work on), rate the priority level for each one. **1** = High priority **2** = Medium priority **3** = Low priority Circle your rankings
	c. We are clear on the critical questions that drive our collaboration, d. Our collaborative work is monitored and supported. 13. We have identified and honored the commitments we have made to the members of our collaborative teams in order to enhance the effectiveness of our team. These articulated collective commitments or norms have clarified expectations of how our team will operate, and we use them to address problems that may occur on the team.	A B C D A B C D	1 2 3 1 2 3
6. We assess our effectiveness on the basis of results rather than intentions.	14. The members of each of our collaborative teams are working interdependently to achieve one or more SMART goals that align with our school goals. Each team has identified		

40

	specific action steps members will take to achieve the goal and a process for monitoring progress toward the goal. The identification and pursuit of SMART goals by each collaborative team are critical elements of the school's continuous improvement process.	A	B	C	D	1	2	3
7. Individuals, teams, and schools seek relevant data and information and use it to promote continuous improvement.	15. Collaborative teams of teachers regard ongoing analysis of evidence of student learning as a critical element in the teaching and learning process. Teachers are provided with frequent and timely information regarding the achievement of their students. They use that information to	A	B	C	D	1	2	3
	a. Respond to students who are experiencing difficulty, b. Enrich and extend the learning of students who are proficient, c. Inform and improve the individual and collective practice of members, d. Indentify team professional development needs, and e. Measure progress toward team goals.							
8. The central office leadership provides the clear parameters and priorities, ongoing support, systems for monitoring progress, and sustained focus essential to	16. The District has demonstrated a sustained commitment to improving schools by developing the capacity of school personnel to function as a PLC. District leaders have been explicit about specific practices they expect to see in each school, have created processes to support principals in							

(Continued)

Figure 4.1 (Continued)

Elements of a Professional Learning Community	Indicators of a Professional Learning Community	Rate **A** = N/A; doesn't fit **B** = We need to work on this! **C** = Partially in place, occasional **D** = In place, frequently observed Circle your ratings	Prioritize Of those rated **B** (partially in place) or **C** (need to work on), rate the priority level for each one. **1** = High priority **2** = Medium priority **3** = Low priority Circle your rankings
implementing the professional learning community process in schools throughout the district.	implementing those practices, and monitor the progress of implementation.	A B C D	
9. We have established processes for addressing conflict, and use conflict as a tool for learning together in order to improve our school.	17. Members of the staff recognize that conflict is an essential and inevitable by-product of a successful substantive change effort. They have thoughtfully and purposefully created processes to help use conflict as a tool for learning together and improving the school.	A B C D	1 2 3 1 2 3

In your own words, briefly describe your school's Greatest Area of Need (GAN) in the space below.

Source: Adapted and modified from DuFour, DuFour, Eaker, and Many (2010).

common assessments, and sample pyramids of intervention were also gathered at each school site. Based on the teacher interviews, analysis of the data, and review of the artifacts, a report summarizing what was found was written and published. Tools for summarizing the data are shown in Figures 4.2, 4.3, and 4.4.

As teachers and principals examined the feedback generated by their own reflections, they identified several potential areas for improvement. Many buildings recognized the need to build shared knowledge of PLC structures before making meaningful changes in their practice. Other schools identified the need for common language regarding important cultural and structural aspects of a PLC. Still other schools set out to create agreement on the questions fundamental to the daily work of PLCs: What should students know and be able to do as a result of this class, how will we know they have learned what was expected, and how will we respond when they do or do not learn what was expected?

Responding to the findings of the reflective audit

Like all states' education departments, the Louisiana State Department of Education had developed an exhaustive set of grade-level expectations, but teachers in Allen Parish found there simply wasn't enough time in the school day, school year, or a student's academic career to ensure mastery of so many standards. Based on the feedback generated during the reflective audit, teachers worked to identify a manageable number of what Doug Reeves called *power standards* (2002, p. 110)—the essential outcomes all teachers would ensure their students learned—and labeled them as *Power GLEs* (grade-level expectations).

Clarity around the Power GLEs created momentum for the development of a balanced and coherent system of assessment. As a result of the audit process, teachers realized that assessment in Allen Parish relied almost exclusively on summative assessments. The teachers worked to develop more frequent and formative assessments that identified which students needed more time and support, and they guided collaborative teams toward aspects of their instructional practice that needed improvement.

The faculty embraced common assessments that were more frequent and formative. Teams began to use assessments created by teams of teachers, connected to the Power GLEs, and administered at the same time to all students enrolled in the same class, course, or grade level. With agreement in place on *what* students should learn and ways to determine *how* well they had learned it, teachers turned their attention to the creation of schoolwide and systematic pyramids of intervention.

Figure 4.2 Survey Tally Sheet

Essential Elements of a Professional Learning Community Greatest Area of Need Tally Sheet

PLC Element	1	1	1	2	2	3	3	3	4	4	5	5	6	7	8	9
PLC Indicator	1	2	3	4	5	6	7	8	9	10	11	12	13	14	15	16	17
A																	
B-1																	
B-2																	
B-3																	
C-1																	
C-2																	
C-3																	
D																	

Figure 4.3   Directions for Using the Priority Grid

1. Write the topics considered for prioritization in the blank spaces.

2. Go to the box with 1 and 2 entered under the large 1 in the upper left of the grid. Circle the number of the topic to which you give greater priority, 1 or 2.

3. Move down to the box with 1 and 3 entered and circle your topic priority. Continue circling your priorities down through the box with 1 and 17.

4. Move up the column under the large 2 and go to the box with 2 and 3 entered and circle your topic priority.

5. Continue this process with the boxes containing the numbers through 17. Doing so will have you comparing each topic to every other topic in pairs.

6. Go to the bottom of the page and indicate the number of times you have circled each number. This determines your final rankings. The more times an item is circled, the greater its priority.

 © Kildeer Countryside Community Consolidated School District 96 May be used for training or educational purposes

Teachers and principals considered many ideas as Allen Parish set out to create effective intervention plans. Not only did the presence of interventions benefit students, it also changed the culture of the schools. Imagine students' reactions when it became clear that they were *required* to complete their homework and were *required* to attend tutorial sessions if they were not successful. The interventions conveyed the powerful message that learning was not optional. It was required!

The impact of reflecting on our practice

As significant as the structural changes were, the cultural shifts were even more dramatic. Participating in the reflective audit process brought teachers together to "challenge and question each other's practice in spirited but optimistic ways" (Andy Hargreaves as quoted in Sparks, 2004, p. 48).

When asked what had changed since the PLC initiative had begun, one teacher replied that it was easier to describe what had *not* changed. She explained, "Gone are the days when I teach/you teach. Now 'WE' teach all students no matter what the subject matter." Another teacher reported relationships were far more professional and focused on student learning. "Our conversations are very different," she said. "We talk about learning everywhere; in the teacher's lounge, on the sidewalk before and after school, through emails and phone calls," she continued. "Our conversations are more focused on how to improve student work, and we spend much less time complaining" (personal communication, October, 2004).

Figure 4.4 Grid for Prioritizing Areas of Greatest Need

Priority Grid

Kildeer Countryside CCSD 96
Maybe used for training or educational purposes

Start Here

1																	
1 2	**2**																
1 3	2 3	**3**															
1 4	2 4	3 4	**4**														
1 5	2 5	3 5	4 5	**5**													
1 6	2 6	3 6	4 6	5 6	**6**												
1 7	2 7	3 7	4 7	5 7	6 7	**7**											
1 8	2 8	3 8	4 8	5 8	6 8	7 8	**8**										
1 9	2 9	3 9	4 9	5 9	6 9	7 9	8 9	**9**									
1 10	2 10	3 10	4 10	5 10	6 10	7 10	8 10	9 10	**10**								
1 11	2 11	3 11	4 11	5 11	6 11	7 11	8 11	9 11	10 11	**11**							
1 12	2 12	3 12	4 12	5 12	6 12	7 12	8 12	9 12	10 12	11 12	**12**						
1 13	2 13	3 13	4 13	5 13	6 13	7 13	8 13	9 13	10 13	11 13	12 13	**13**					
1 14	2 14	3 14	4 14	5 14	6 14	7 14	8 14	9 14	10 14	11 14	12 14	13 14	**14**				
1 15	2 15	3 15	4 15	5 15	6 15	7 15	8 15	9 15	10 15	11 15	12 15	13 15	14 15	**15**			
1 16	2 16	3 16	4 16	5 16	6 16	7 16	8 16	9 16	10 16	11 16	12 16	13 16	14 16	15 16	**16**		
1 17	2 17	3 17	4 17	5 17	6 17	7 17	8 17	9 17	10 17	11 17	12 17	13 17	14 17	15 17	16 17	**17**	
1 18	2 18	3 18	4 18	5 18	6 18	7 18	8 18	9 18	10 18	11 18	12 18	13 18	14 18	15 18	16 18	17 18	

TOTALS:

1	2	3	4	5	6	7	8	9	10	11	12	13	14	15	16	17	18

Principals reported that teachers no longer felt isolated or left alone to solve problems. As one principal remarked, "Our teachers realize they can bring their challenges to a group of fellow teachers and work together." He continued:

> Teachers meet to examine student work and talk about strategies for re-teaching. We share a common goal that all our students will succeed and sometimes that means having to admit something doesn't work or accepting advice from others. That did not happen before we began working as a PLC. (personal communication, October, 2004)

The cultural shifts were not confined to teachers and principals; parents also viewed the school differently. As one staff member reported,

> Parents are seeing interventions and appreciate the extra time spent with any students who need extra help. They appreciate that teachers are working together for the good of all students and realize school is an important part of their children's lives. Parents see the entire faculty as having the children's best interests at heart and support the changes we are trying to make. (personal communication, October, 2004)

Reflecting on their practice moved Allen Parish from conversation to action, from theory to practice, from knowing to *doing*. As teachers responded to the findings of the reflective audit process, they acquired a deeper understanding of PLC practices, accepted the need for structural changes, and committed to developing collaborative teams, essential outcomes, common assessments, and pyramids of intervention. These changes were implemented more effectively and efficiently than before.

Look for the leverage points

Reflecting on our practice—often called making meaning of our practice—is a high-leverage strategy. Sometimes we assume the PLC model is more deeply embedded than it really is, but if principals can identify key leverage points, they can dramatically accelerate their school improvement efforts.

Many educators in Allen Parish were aware of the benefits of PLCs, but schools had made only halting progress toward becoming PLCs. This changed when they examined their work through the lens of the reflective audit. The process took the better part of an entire school year, but only after consciously reflecting on their work did they begin to clarify the essential curriculum, gather data about student progress, and implement systematic schoolwide pyramids of intervention.

As teachers and principals reviewed the results of the reflective audit process, they developed a deeper understanding of the conceptual framework of PLCs. Teachers and principals openly and publicly examined specific recommendations, implemented new procedures, focused on goal setting, and celebrated short-term success. In short, they changed the culture of their schools in powerful ways and began to behave differently.

One of the key leverage points for principals in Allen Parish was the gathering of artifacts or work products. Principals became more aware of the level of PLC implementation in their schools by requiring each team to produce a portfolio of work products and artifacts for each of the three big ideas of a PLC.

Examples of artifacts collected as evidence of a Focus on Learning included (1) a list of the Power GLEs and pacing guides for each grade level, (2) copies of team-developed common assessments and data analysis reports, and (3) descriptions of how each team was systematically providing time for remediation, extension, and enrichment.

Collecting artifacts also helped principals understand the current level of collaboration in each school by making the team norms and SMART goals public. Evidence about how teams were organized, when they were provided with time to meet, and how the work of the teams was monitored and supported was also gathered.

Finally, principals were able to assess their schools' Results Orientation by collecting examples of how data generated by common assessments was presented to and used by each teacher. Further insights were gained by reviewing data analysis sheets that identified the teams' conclusions and strategies for improvement.

In Allen Parish, educators recognized their efforts were worthwhile, and the results significant. During a three-year period beginning in 2002, student achievement improved by 37%, and the Allen Parish schools rose from the third to first quartile in state rankings. Allen Parish was recognized as one of the top ten school systems in the state when measured by the amount of improvement in the level of student achievement.

IDENTIFYING LEVERAGE POINTS IN A PLC

Participating in the reflective audit—making meaning of our practice—is an example of a high-leverage strategy, but it was not until principals hit upon the idea of collecting work products and artifacts that the change process accelerated. Collecting artifacts for each of the three big ideas is an example of a leverage point.

Participating in the reflective audit process identified the current reality in Allen Parish schools, clarified what needed to be done to continue the improvement process, and contributed to the successful implementation of PLCs. As Sparks wrote, being clear about the current reality in your school "is essential because individuals and organizations move toward that which they are clearest about. It is very difficult for leaders to lead in the creation of that which they cannot describe in some detail" (2005, p. 148).

Section II

Practical Applications

5 The Secret to Success

Leverage a Focus on Learning

This assertion—the fundamental purpose of the school is to help all students learn the knowledge, skills, and dispositions most essential to their success—is the biggest of the Big Ideas that drive the work of PLCs.

—DuFour, DuFour, & Eaker (2008, p. 118)

The essence of Professional Learning Communities (PLCs) is captured by three big ideas, and as principals work to develop the first of the three big ideas, a Focus on Learning in their schools, they attempt to answer four critical questions of learning:

1. *What do we want our children to know and be able to do?* Answering this initial question requires that faculty reach agreement on what teachers will teach and students will learn. The first question calls for teams to develop great clarity and a deep understanding of which standards are essential for every to child learn.

2. *How will we know they have learned?* Tackling the second question compels teachers to develop balanced and coherent systems of assessment. These systems must generate timely and accurate information about how students are progressing through the curriculum while creating rich and varied data to drive decisions about how to teach more effectively.

3. *What will we do when they have not learned?* Responding to Question 3 means that teams provide more time and support for students who have not yet learned what was expected. When students do not succeed, teachers in a PLC raise the level of support rather than lower expectations. They believe all kids can learn—given enough time and support—and act in accordance with that belief.

4. *What will we do when students have learned?* Addressing the final question necessitates that teachers provide enriched and/or expanded learning opportunities for students who have been successful and learned what was expected. It is essential that students continue to learn and progress, even if they have already demonstrated they are proficient on a particular standard.

WHAT MATTERS MOST

In recent years, a tremendous amount of attention has been devoted to the Common Core State Standards (CCSS), but talking about standards is not a new conversation. The first call for rigorous standards came in 1989, when President George H. W. Bush convened a national summit on education. One of the outcomes of that conference was the goal that all children in grades 4, 8, and 12 would demonstrate mastery on a challenging set of standards common to all school districts in the nation. Over the next 10 years, federal policy continued to encourage and provide incentives for the development of standards in all 50 states. This trend continued and was reinforced with the passage of the No Child Left Behind Act in 2002.

Construction of a more consistent and comprehensive set of standards began in 2009, and by 2012, a total of 46 states had adopted all or part of the Common Core State Standards. Most recognized that the new standards were better than anything produced by previous state and local initiatives, which generated long lists of standards that were too numerous, too complex, and too varied from place to place. The new CCSS improved on every one of those deficit areas and also responded to the need for a narrower focus and better alignment with curriculum and assessments. Still, and despite all these significant improvements, there were concerns.

The truth is that states, districts, and schools have had standards in one form or another for decades, and the CCSS are simply one more standards initiative in a long line of standards initiatives. This is not a criticism of the CCSS. Make no mistake: The Common Core State Standards are an improvement over past efforts, and they are a step in the right direction. No, the concern is not with the CCSS standards. The concern is with the way school districts are approaching implementation of the CCSS standards and the fact that what many systems are doing today differs very little from the way this task was approached in the past.

The reason prior standards initiatives failed to reach their full potential was less about the standards themselves—there was lots about the old standards that was pretty good—and more about how teachers interacted with the standards. It is unfortunate, but unless we embrace the CCSS differently this time around, it is likely we will have another set of standards in the future.

Common misconceptions about the Common Core State Standards

Too many districts mistake the Common Core State Standards for a curriculum. Most teachers believe there are still too many standards; while there will be some who will try to cover them all, most teachers will not be able teach them all to mastery. Even if teachers could teach them all, there are concerns about our collective ability to adequately assess them all and even less confidence about the ability to effectively remediate them all.

Too many districts also mistake the CCSS for an instructional strategy. What should be obvious to everyone by now is that standards don't teach; teachers do. While the CCSS can help guide instruction, teachers still need to decide what students should know and be able to do. According to recent surveys conducted by Kober and Rentner (2011, 2012), the biggest barriers to successful implementation of the CCSS were finding enough time to do the work and finding sufficient funding to support the necessary professional development.

Perhaps worst of all, too many administrators are relying on the Common Core State Standards as *the* vehicle to improve student achievement in their schools. We often hear the CCSS referred to as the guaranteed and viable curriculum and that all of the individual standards are of equal importance. Too many district-level leaders believe distributing a prepackaged list of standards, learning targets, and "I can" statements developed by the state department of education or a national testing company will somehow improve student learning. To paraphrase the late, great Yogi Berra, this approach is "déjà vu all over again."

Far too many teachers in far too many schools are being asked—even required—to implement the CCSS without the opportunity to thoroughly understand the standards. People support that which they help create so, the more important question to ask is "Have teachers—the ones responsible for delivering the guaranteed and viable curriculum—been involved in developing, deciding, and designing the guaranteed and viable curriculum, or have they been handed a list of standards that were developed, decided, and designed by someone else?"

Using an approach that emphasizes compliance and alignment over commitment and engagement did not work before, and will not work now. In order for the CCSS to fulfill their promise, principals must engage the faculty in a collaborative process to deeply understand the rigor, content, and connection of one CCSS standard to another. Furthermore, principals must recognize and respond to the effect adopting the CCSS will have on instructional practice.

We must acknowledge that the CCSS are a tool—albeit a great tool—that can enable students to reach increasingly higher levels of learning. The consensus is that the CCSS are more rigorous, more comprehensive, and more aligned than any set of standards developed thus far. Nonetheless, they remain standards and are best thought of as a tool or resource principals and teachers can use to improve student learning.

CREATING AN OPERATIONAL DEFINITION OF WHAT IS ESSENTIAL

Educators across the country have found that one of the most effective and efficient ways to promote a Focus on Learning is by participating in a collaborative process to identify what is most essential for all students to know and be able to do. Prioritizing the standards is an example of a high-leverage strategy principals use to improve their schools.

Despite near universal agreement that there is too much to teach, one of the biggest fears of teachers is that they won't cover everything. Yet in system after system, teachers are told students are tested for all the standards, and thus, all the standards are equally important. This position creates tremendous pressure to "cover" all the standards, but teachers understand that "teaching" the curriculum is different from "covering" the curriculum, and a guaranteed and viable curriculum requires that the standards be taught to mastery.

As one teacher said, "The list of what I am supposed to cover just seems to grow and grow. More than that, what is important today is different from what was important yesterday. How am I supposed to know where to begin?" (personal communication, 2012). Teachers routinely ask themselves the same questions: Are some standards more important than others? Which standards will students need in the next class, course, or grade level? Will all the standards be tested?

In response to this quandary, Heidi Hayes-Jacobs urges teachers to look critically at what matters most. She says,

> Given the limited time you [teachers] have with your students, curriculum design has become more and more an issue of deciding what you won't teach as well as what you will teach. You cannot do it all.

As a designer, you must choose the essential. (Jacobs as quoted in Ainsworth, 2003, p. 14)

Question 1: What do we want students to know and be able to do?

When teachers in traditional schools begin the process of deciding what is essential, they are often asked, "What do you teach?" or "What do you spend the most time teaching?" or even "What do you like to teach?" Sometimes teachers describe their essential learning targets in terms of the topics they cover or questions they must prepare their students for on the state tests.

But, these are the wrong answers—or maybe the right answers to the wrong questions. Jeanne Spiller suggests that instead of asking teachers to describe what they *teach*, principals should ask teachers to define what their students should *learn* (personal communication, October 2006). The process of identifying what is essential—what all students must learn and be able to do as a result of a class, a course, or a grade level—should reflect a Focus on Learning, not teaching.

When Spiller works with teachers, she begins with some guiding questions to help focus their attention on what is essential. For example, she asks teachers to identify which standards—according to state and local assessment data—they need to emphasize. Which standards represent concepts and skills that reflect endurance, have leverage, require a certain level of readiness, and will be assessed? She continues using a simple six-step process to identify what is essential for each class, course, or grade level (personal communication, October 2006).

Step 1: You Decide

Take five minutes and, on your own, quickly mark each standard you consider absolutely essential for student success in your class, course, or grade level.

Step 2: Table Talk

Talk to your colleagues and note where you agree, disagree, or are not sure. Use common and consistent criteria to help you decide what is essential for your students to know and be able to do.

Step 3: Consult Testing Guides and Data

Review any available data (such as item analysis reports) to look for concepts and skills that are weak or emphasized on the test(s). Identify how many questions and what type of questions were asked for each of the various concepts and skills. Revise your selections for what is essential based on your review of the test data and the related information.

Step 4: Chart Selections as a Team

Record the group's consensus of what is essential for all students to learn on pieces of chart paper.

Step 5: Share Team Selections and Seek Consensus

Post each team's selections (on chart paper) next to one another. Reach initial consensus on what is essential for all students to know and be able to do.

Step 6: Check Vertical Alignment, Gaps, Overlaps, and Omissions

Post your charts on the wall in order. Look vertically for the flow within and between the classes, courses, or grade levels. Look for and identify any gaps, overlaps, and omissions.

The process of deciding what is essential for students to learn requires teachers to ask themselves what is important enough to teach, assess, and reteach if necessary. The research is clear. Students will learn more if the expectations for learning are clearly defined, if students know in advance the criteria for meeting those expectations, and if instruction and assessment support those expectations.

If everything is important, then nothing is important

The importance of helping teams reach consensus around what is essential became clear during a recent team meeting when teachers were given a sample unit plan and asked to "identify what was important for students to learn" before an upcoming assessment. Teachers embraced the task, but as they worked to identify the requisite standards for the upcoming unit, it became obvious that each individual was using her or his own unique criteria to prioritize what was essential for students to learn. The result was several different and competing sets of essential outcomes based on the different views of individual teachers. Agreement on the unit's essential outcomes remained an elusive goal.

Larry Ainsworth (2013) argues that this kind of dilemma is not unique to a single district, school, or team. He suggests,

Left to their own professional opinions when faced with the task of narrowing a voluminous number of student learning outcomes, educators naturally pick and choose those they know best, like best, the ones for which they have materials and lesson plans or activities, and those most likely to appear on state tests." (p. 16)

Reaching consensus on essential outcomes is important, but many teachers wonder where to begin the task of prioritizing such an overwhelming number of standards. Should teachers be allowed to prioritize the standards? Educators on both sides of this question make passionate arguments for and against the idea of prioritizing standards. But, whether we acknowledge it or not, teachers are identifying what is essential and prioritizing standards all the time. For them, it is a practical necessity. To paraphrase the famous quote, "If everything is a priority, then nothing is a priority."

Thus, the question is not whether teachers will prioritize the standards but how teachers will prioritize the standards. Will they prioritize the standards using a formal or informal process? Will they work in isolation or in collaboration with others? Will they use a unique set of criteria that is different for each individual teacher or a common and agreed-upon set of criteria developed while working as a team?

In response to this predicament, Ted Horrell and his colleagues in Shelby County, Tennessee, translated criteria first developed by Reeves (2002, p. 110) and later modified by Ainsworth (2013, p. 26) into an easy to remember acronym. Using the REAL criteria (Readiness, Endurance, Assessed, and Leverage), teachers collaborate around whether a particular standard should be considered a priority. An example for each of the four categories follows.

Readiness

The R stands for Readiness. A standard selected under this criterion provides students with essential knowledge and skills necessary for success in the next class, course, or grade level. Here is an example of a Readiness standard:

Algebra I Standard: Manipulate formulas and solve literal equations.

Student proficiency on this standard is necessary for success in subsequent math classes, including Geometry and Algebra II. Students who cannot demonstrate these skills would not be ready to advance to the next level of instruction.

Endurance

The *E* represents Endurance. A standard selected under this criterion provides students with knowledge and skills that are useful beyond a single test or unit of study. Here is an example of an Endurance standard:

> English 9–10 Standard: Determine a central idea of a text, and analyze its development over the course of the text, including how it emerges and is shaped and refined by specific details; provide an objective summary of the text.

This standard, in particular the skill of providing an objective summary of written passages, will be required for future high school and college courses. It is also likely to be an essential skill in many professions and in everyday life. The standard has a high degree of endurance.

Assessed

The *A* represents Assessed. Standards selected under this criterion are those that will be assessed on upcoming state and national exams. Here is an example of a standard reflecting the Assessed criterion:

> Algebra I Standard: Order and classify rational numbers.

Although ordering numbers is a vital part of the math curriculum that most students master at an early age, classifying rational numbers is not a skill that is an essential building block for understanding future concepts, nor does it have much practical application outside of the math curriculum. However, there are questions on the ACT and the PSAT that require students to use this specific skill—a fact that would have to be considered when prioritizing this standard.

Leverage

The *L* corresponds to Leverage. Standards selected under this criterion will provide students with knowledge and skills that will be of value in multiple disciplines. Here is an example of a standard reflecting the Leverage criterion:

> Physical Science Standard: Choose, construct, and analyze appropriate graphical representations for a data set.

Though it is part of the physical science curriculum, this standard has significant leverage. Students will be expected to apply these skills in future science classes as well as in other content areas such as social studies, career and technical education, and mathematics.

Benefits of prioritizing the standards

Principals recognize that one of the most important benefits of prioritizing the standards is that the process shifts the conversation of a teacher in a school, in a department, or on a team from teaching to learning. Agreement on what is essential helps teachers focus their time and expertise on specific outcomes that will be most beneficial to students.

With agreement in place on what matters most, teachers can be assured that they are applying their energy to what is absolutely essential to student success in the classroom and beyond. As Doug Reeves says, "Teaching the power [priority] standards for depth of understanding will do more to prepare students for success; not only on the state test, but in school and life as well" (2002, p. 99).

Once faculty and staff agree on what is essential, teachers become more comfortable with the idea that if they do not cover ever single standard, the students are not missing something important. Ainsworth argues that a carefully articulated set of prioritized standards will address the overwhelming majority (88%) of what is typically covered on most state tests (2003, p. 97) and represents "the safety net of standards each teacher needs to make sure every student learns prior to leaving the current grade" (2003, p. 111).

According to Ainsworth, "The consensus among educators nationwide is that in-depth instruction of 'essential' concepts and skills is more effective than superficially 'covering' every concept in the textbook" (2003, p. 7). Prioritizing the standards encourages teachers to embrace more effective instructional practices by reducing the pressure to cover the material.

Identifying what is essential helps minimize the fear that a standards-based curriculum will somehow standardize teaching. A set of prioritized standards identifies what the curriculum will be, but it is up to teachers to determine how to present the essential material most effectively. Nothing in the process of prioritizing standards dictates pedagogy or limits a teacher's academic freedom. As Reeves argues, the process of prioritizing standards "does not limit teachers' ability to draw upon their own individual talents, insights, expertise, and creativity to help their students deeply grasp the knowledge and skills they need to know" (as quoted in Ainsworth, 2003, p. 98)

Collaboratively prioritizing the standards creates greater clarity around what teachers should teach and students should learn. Many teachers find the process allows them to see how one standard overlaps with other standards. Furthermore, prioritizing the standards sharpens the focus on what students should learn, which promotes development of better assessments and helps identify which students will need more time and support. This kind of knowledge fosters more effective planning and more efficient sharing of resources.

Perhaps the biggest argument in favor of prioritizing standards is the positive effect the process has on sharpening the pedagogy and deepening the content knowledge of teachers. Teams who prioritize the standards recognize that in many ways, the process is as important as the product. Carefully analyzing the standards, debating the merits of individual standards, and coming to consensus on what is most essential help everyone gain a more thorough understanding of what teachers should teach and students should learn.

The choice to engage teachers in a process that promotes a deep understanding of the standards will yield far better results than any effort to align teachers to a set of standards developed by the state department of education or outside publisher. In its simplest terms, prioritizing standards creates an operational definition for what is essential. Not only will students benefit from a focused, cohesive, and well-articulated curriculum, but teachers will benefit as well. By collaborating and agreeing on what is essential, principals and teachers take a significant step toward a Focus on Learning.

Question 2: How do we know students have learned?

Generating a continuous flow of information regarding student progress and the effectiveness of instructional strategies is another way principals can generate a sharper Focus on Learning and improve their schools.

Principals must consider two priorities when aligning their school's assessment practices. First, they must ensure that whatever assessment system is in place, it reflects a balance of both formative and summative assessment. Second, they must ensure that those using the system understand and utilize the assessments for their intended purposes. Both of these are ideas essential to the creation of the Balanced and Coherent System of Assessment

THE BALANCED AND COHERENT SYSTEM OF ASSESSMENT: PROVIDING A STEADY STREAM OF INFORMATION

> *As we look to the future, we must balance annual, interim or benchmark, and classroom assessment. Only then will we meet the critically important information needs of all instructional decision makers.*

> —Stiggins, 2007, p. 29

As Stiggins suggests, principals need to take advantage of multiple types of assessments to provide teachers with the data they need to make decisions about student learning. Based on his advice, relying on any one, single method of assessment would not represent what we have come to understand as best practice in developing an effective assessment system. The most successful principals understand the best assessment systems balance data from both formative and summative assessments and use information from multiple sources to manage and monitor student learning.

Principals also understand the importance of bringing coherence, clarity, and understanding to the assessment practices in their school. In and of themselves, assessments are neither formative nor summative, and one method is not inherently better or worse than the other. What determines whether, and to what degree, a test is formative or summative is the way teachers use the results. It is important that teachers understand the purpose of formative and summative assessments and use assessment data appropriately.

One resource that has been helpful in assisting teachers to understand the various dimensions of assessment is the Balanced and Coherent System of Assessment model, as shown in Figure 5.1. The Balanced and Coherent model illustrates the relationship between formative and summative assessment and promotes coherence by defining the role that data from different types of assessment play in promoting higher levels of student learning.

The model describes four categories of assessment arranged along a continuum from most formative to most summative. The four categories—shown from left to right in the figure—are labeled Classroom Assessments (most formative), Common Assessments (more formative), District-Level or Benchmark Assessments (more summative), and External Assessments (most summative). All four categories of assessment are valid when used for the right purpose.

Most formative assessments

These ongoing, continuous, sometimes in-the-moment assessments occur daily at the classroom level. In addition to verbal responses, teachers may use whiteboards, exit slips, hand signals, or colored cups as tools to check for understanding during the course of their regular classroom instruction. These assessments are rarely graded and are intended to provide teachers with the kind of highly formative feedback advocated by authors such as Rick Stiggins, Jan Chappuis, and Dylan William.

In his book *The Mega System*, Sam Redding (2006) describes the kinds of assessments in the most formative category as "quick diagnostic tests

Figure 5.1 A Balanced and Coherent System of Assessment

Classroom Assessments	Common Assessments	District Level Assessments	External Assessments
Most Formative	More Formative	More Summative	Most Summative
Daily	Weekly / Unit	Monthly / Semester	Annual
Ongoing Student and Teacher Formative Assessment	Collaboratively Developed CFAs	Collaboratively Developed DBAs	Annual State Mandated Summative Assessment
Diagnostic and Prescriptive	Identify Students Eligible for Support in a Pyramid of Interventions	Calibrate and Pace the Curriculum	Ranks and Benchmarks Entrance and Exit Criteria
		Identify Students Eligible for Ongoing Remedial and Programmatic Support	

Source: Kildeer Countryside CCSD. Used with permission.

used to prescribe appropriate learning activities for a student or group of students." He elaborates, "These tests may be pencil-and-paper tests, oral quizzes, or 'show-me' assessments that a teacher can quickly and conveniently administer to determine the level of an individual student's mastery of the lesson's objectives" (Redding, 2006, p. 87).

Most summative assessments

At the opposite end of the spectrum is the category representing most summative assessments. One of the best examples of assessments in this category is the once-a-year, high-stakes, state-sponsored examinations so prevalent in American public schools. Interestingly, James Popham (2008) suggests that, while these annual assessments may play an important role in monitoring student progress and providing system-level information for policymakers, there is no evidence that such assessments increase student achievement.

Within the most summative assessment category, Redding includes "state assessments and norm-referenced achievement tests that provide an annual assessment of each student's and school's progress by subject area and grade level" (2006, p. 88). These assessments provide a basis for comparing an individual student's performance with that of a larger group. They help schools or districts target areas in which groups of students may be underperforming but do not provide teachers with the kind of timely information they need in making instructional decisions that help individual students learn. Teachers understand that for their students, receiving feedback on progress only once a year, no matter how valid or reliable, is not enough.

Harnessing the power of interim assessments:
More formative and more summative assessments

Assessments from the two categories on either ends of the continuum are the most common examples found in schools, but it is the assessments found in between these categories—what we have labeled as the more formative and more summative assessments—that offer teachers and principals the biggest opportunity to impact student learning. Kim Marshall (2006) describes these assessments as interim assessments and argues that interim assessments "represent the most powerful entry point for those principals determined to improve instruction and boost student achievement" (p. 4).

Sometimes labeled common formative, common summative, or district benchmark assessments, the assessments in the middle of the model share some characteristics; however, certain aspects about frequency, focus, and purpose help differentiate one from another. Understanding the similarities and differences of the two categories brings coherence to the system.

Principals often use data from assessments in the more formative category to support intervention decisions and identify the most effective teaching practices. Principals can use the data generated by assessments in the more summative category to monitor the pace of instruction and determine whether students have retained mastery of essential learnings. On a very practical level, using assessments in the middle of the assessment continuum helps principals manage and monitor teaching and learning throughout the school.

More summative assessments: Using periodic assessments to manage and monitor learning

Sam Redding (2006) suggests that assessments in the more summative category be linked to grading periods and administered to students in the same class, course, or grade level two, three, or four times a year, depending on whether schools report student progress to parents using a semester, trimester, or quarterly schedule.

Teachers can use data from more summative assessments to generate grades and to align instruction with the annual, high-stakes assessments. Teachers can also use data from these more summative assessments to establish a context for calibrating pacing guides, setting proficiency targets, and monitoring mastery of content introduced earlier in the year.

A pacing guide reflects the best thinking of a textbook publisher, central office administrator, or committee of teachers, but the typical guide has one glaring weakness: It lacks a context for determining if the recommended pace of instruction is appropriate. Linking assessment results with the pacing guide provide this much needed context. When teachers specify the level of proficiency they expect students to attain, results of the periodic assessments can be used to compare the expected level of achievement with the attained level.

Assume that a school has decided that 80% of the students should demonstrate mastery on 80% of the learning targets within a unit of study. If 80% of the students correctly answered at least 80% of the questions on the quarterly assessment, the principal can be confident that the curriculum is being delivered at an appropriate pace. If, on the other hand, only 60% of the students answered at least 80% of the items correctly, it could be that the pace of instruction is too fast or that teachers are attempting to cover too much information. Likewise, if 100% of the students answered at least 80% of the questions correctly, it may be that the pace of instruction is too slow and can be accelerated. Using the results of periodic assessments can help principals determine if the recommendations in the pacing guide are realistic, achievable, and appropriate for their students. The assessment results create the context by which the faculty and staff determine whether or not the *pace of instruction* is appropriate.

Data from more summative assessments also allows teachers to monitor mastery of content introduced earlier in the year. Assessments in the more summative category generate evidence that students have or have not retained previous learning. If the level of mastery begins to erode, teachers can reteach and reinforce important content before any learning gaps become problematic. As an example, consider how a quarterly assessment can be used to check the level of mastery at the end of a nine-week period.

Using the recommendation of no more than 8 to 10 standards per subject, per semester, teams of teachers design an assessment consisting of five questions for each of four learning targets, so, in this example, the first quarter assessment would consist of 20 items. Since the team has previously defined proficiency as correctly answering at least four of the five questions—80%—for each target, teachers identify which students are and are not proficient based on the results of their assessment.

At the end of the second quarter, teachers again design an assessment to check the level of mastery of the second-quarter learning targets using approximately 20 questions (five questions for each of four targets). However, in addition to the 20 questions that reflect the learning targets for second quarter, teachers select five questions that reflect curriculum taught earlier in the year. The five questions—representing essential outcomes from the first quarter—are added to the 20 questions designed to measure the second-quarter learning targets, making the second-quarter exam 25 questions long.

The process repeats itself in each subsequent quarter. For the third quarter, roughly four or five third-quarter learning targets are assessed with four to five questions each, forming a core of 20 questions for the third-quarter assessment. Five questions from the first quarter and five more questions from the second quarter are added to check whether students are still proficient on the targets taught earlier in the year. The bulk of the third-quarter assessment—now 30 questions long—consists of items designed to assess the third-quarter targets, but a select number of additional items are designed to monitor mastery of learning targets taught earlier in the year.

By adding questions that reflect the essential learning targets from previous grading periods, teachers gather important information on whether or not students have maintained previous levels of mastery. If mastery begins to erode, or if skills become rusty, teachers can intervene before deficits grow.

Teachers find data generated by assessments in the more summative category to be more useful than once-a-year autopsy data generated by state tests. However, assessments in this category also have some limitations. The biggest limit is that assessments given every quarter, trimester, or semester are not timely enough to drive the kind of instructional decision making critical to improving student learning. Teachers need more frequent assessments to (1) identify students by name and need who will require more time and support to become proficient and (2) identify which instructional practices most effectively promoted higher levels of learning. Principals can address both of these goals by encouraging the use of assessments from the more formative category of the Balanced and Coherent System of Assessment.

More formative assessments: Providing a steady stream of information about student learning

Carol Ann Tomlinson captured the essence of why the more formative category of assessments are so valuable to teachers when she observed, "I came to understand that assessments that came at the end of a unit [more summative assessments]—although important manifestations of student knowledge, understanding, and skill—were less useful to me as a teacher than were assessments that occurred *during* a unit of study" (2007/2008, p. 11). To maximize the impact of instruction, teachers need a steady flow of timely and accurate information about student learning.

Sam Redding described more formative assessments as embedded activities that are "aligned to objectives with criteria for mastery which enable a teacher to check student progress within the context of instruction." He continued, saying, "By successfully completing the assigned activities, students demonstrate a level of mastery of the objectives that the activities are designed to teach or to reinforce" (2006, p. 88).

Typically designed by teams of teachers at the building level, embedded assessments fall on the formative side of the continuum. They are given on a more frequent basis to students taking the same class or course, or at the same grade level, and they serve a different purpose than the more summative assessments described previously. Embedded assessments provide useful information to collaborative teams, because they are closely linked to what is being taught, provide a consistent standard of comparison between classrooms, and generate results that are timely enough to allow for adjustments during the instruction sequence.

Teams use these assessments to identify which students, by name and need, will require additional time and support to reach proficiency. Student responses on frequent assessments provide teachers with the data they need to create meaningful intervention programs. These short-cycle assessments are also powerful sources of information about the effectiveness of a teacher's instructional practices. As Carol Ann Tomlinson observed, "The greatest power of assessment information lies in its capacity to help me [the teacher] see how to become a better teacher" (2007/2008, p. 11).

Involving students in a process of writing questions that might be included on the common assessment is an excellent example of a high-leverage strategy that makes assessment part of the learning process. As a leverage point any principal can execute, this idea capitalizes on the nature of the more formative or embedded assessments and provides an authentic way to review and revisit the learning targets students were expected to learn.

In preparation for an upcoming quiz on Friday, the teacher reviews the unit's learning targets and asks each student to develop five questions that might appear on the quiz. The task is assigned to the students as homework on Wednesday night. When the students arrive in class on Thursday, they are organized into groups of four or five and are given time to discuss all of the questions developed by the other members of their group. The goal of each group is to reach agreement on the best three, four, or five questions based on what they believe they were expected to learn. Once a consensus is reached, the group's collaborative effort is submitted to the teacher.

Preparing for the assessment in this way represents a powerful leverage point for any principal interested in improving student achievement. For the teacher, the idea provides an efficient way to create the upcoming assessment. The result of the activity is between 20 and 25 additional items that could be included on an assessment. Some editing and proofreading will inevitably be required, but, when the teacher combines the students' items with items gleaned from other sources, there are more than enough questions to create alternate forms of the test. For students, this activity is an effective way to review for an upcoming assessment. It engages students in their own learning by building ownership of the questions that appear on the quiz, enhances the authenticity of discussions about which questions best match learning targets, and increases the rigor of the task by requiring students to engage in creating potential questions.

The Balanced and Coherent System of Assessment meets the criteria of a high-leverage strategy more completely than nearly any other strategy available to a principal. By leveraging teachers' understanding of the Balanced and Coherent System of Assessment, principals are able to move beyond any potential confusion and take the advantages of several other high-leverage strategies, such as access to timely and accurate information and collaboration.

THE NEED FOR SPEED: CRITERIA FOR DESIGNING EFFECTIVE PYRAMIDS OF INTERVENTION

The SPEED acronym stands for Systematic, Practical, Effective, Essential, and Directive. The SPEED criteria were designed to help guide the development of schoolwide and systematic pyramids of intervention. To further this goal, schools can design a brochure describing the resources available to students as part of the pyramid of intervention. Information in the brochure should be revised annually, and the brochure should be made available to parents at the beginning of each school year. Figures 5.2, 5.3, and 5.4 show examples of brochures from Kildeer Countryside Community Consolidated School District 96 in Buffalo Grove, Illinois.

Developing and discussing the SPEED criteria represents another conscious effort to use high-leverage strategies to improve teaching and learning. When schools develop pyramids of intervention that meet the SPEED criteria, they meet the needs of individual learners, create greater ownership of student learning on the part of the faculty, and maximize the school's available resources. Generating a written product describing a school's pyramid of intervention is an opportunity to build shared knowledge and promote system clarity, and is an important leverage point for principals.

Figure 5.2 Brochure for Kindergarten Interventions

WHAT IS RtI?

Response to Intervention (RtI) is a process designed to help schools focus on high quality interventions that are matched to student needs and monitored on a frequent basis. The information gained from an RtI process is used by school personnel and parents to adapt instruction and to make decisions regarding the student's educational program. Perhaps the greatest benefit of an RtI approach is that it eliminates a "wait to fail" situation because students get help promptly within the general education setting.

Teachers use assessment data to monitor students' progress and make important decisions about what and how to teach children who are not making sufficient progress.

Our RtI system is divided into a four-tier intervention model:

Tier 4: Special Education

Tier 3: Few Students

Tier 2: Some Students

Tier 1: All Students

Tier 1: All Students
Literacy
- Harcourt Trophies Reading Curriculum
- Lucy Calkins Writing Curriculum
- Handwriting Without Tears Curriculum
- Differentiated reading instruction in small groups
- Reading Workshop

Math
- Everyday Mathematics Curriculum
- Differentiated math instruction in small groups

Tier 2: Some Students
All elements of Tier 1, plus:
- Intervention Block targeting areas of literacy, math, speech, and fine motor
- Reading Specialist
- Math Specialist
- Double Dose

Tier 3: Few Students
All elements of Tiers 1 & 2, plus:
- K+ Program

Tier 4: Special Education
- Special Education evaluation
- Integrated Kindergarten
- Special Education resource services

What Is an Intervention?

An intervention exists as an opportunity for a student to receive the extra time and support he or she needs in order to demonstrate content, concept, and skill acquisition relative to the District 96 Curriculum and Framework. Interventions exist within District 96 as part of students' regular school day.

Our students are provided access to academic intervention on an individual basis, demonstrated through performance and assessment. The frequency and intensity of the support is determined by the individual needs of learners. As student need increases, so, too, does the frequency and/or intensity of support. Student progress is monitored regularly. As a student demonstrates proficiency regarding the targeted area of intervention, he or she will be cycled out of the specific intervention.

The SPEED criteria

Systematic

To be systematic, a pyramid of intervention must be schoolwide, independent of an individual teacher, and communicated to everyone (the staff, parents, and students). Furthermore, everyone involved must be able to describe the system of intervention in enough detail that, if and when students need more time and support to learn, teachers and parents know exactly what is available, what needs to happen based on data, who can provide the instruction, and when in the school day the support is available.

Schoolwide, systematic pyramids of intervention provide leveled instruction by increasing the time and intensity of support to struggling students. Effective pyramids of intervention begin with differentiated classroom (core) instruction and increase the time and intensity based on an individual learner's needs. The vast majority of a school's resources are allocated to first instruction, as helping all learners initially will surely limit the number of students who need additional time and support later.

Figure 5.3   Brochure for Elementary Interventions

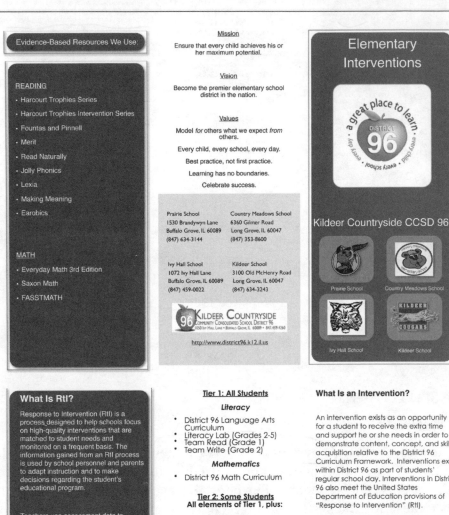

Figure 5.4   Brochure for Middle School Interventions

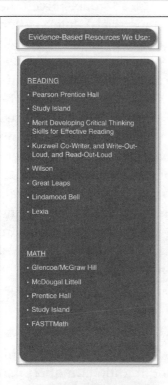

Evidence-Based Resources We Use:

READING
- Pearson Prentice Hall
- Study Island
- Merit Developing Critical Thinking Skills for Effective Reading
- Kurzweil Co-Writer, and Write-Out-Loud, and Read-Out-Loud
- Wilson
- Great Leaps
- Lindamood Bell
- Lexia

MATH
- Glencoe/McGraw Hill
- McDougal Littell
- Prentice Hall
- Study Island
- FASTTMath

Mission
Ensure that every child achieves his or her maximum potential.

Vision
Become the premier elementary school district in the nation.

Values
Model *for* others what we expect *from* others.
Every child, every school, every day.
Best practice, not first practice.
Learning has no boundaries.
Celebrate success.

Twin Groves Middle School
2600 N. Buffalo Grove Road
Buffalo Grove, IL 60089
847-821-8946

Woodlawn Middle School
6362 RFD/Gilmer Road
Long Grove, IL 60047
847-353-8500

www.district96.k12.il.us

Middle School Interventions

Kildeer Countryside CCSD 96

Woodlawn Middle School   Twin Groves Middle School

What is RtI?

Response to Intervention (RtI) is a process designed to help schools focus on high quality interventions that are matched to student needs and monitored on a frequent basis. The information gained from an RtI process is used by school personnel and parents to adapt instruction and to make decisions regarding the student's educational program.

The middle school teachers use assessment data to monitor students' progress and make important decisions about what and how to teach children who are not making sufficient progress.

Our RtI system is divided into a four-tier intervention model:

Tier 4: Special Education
Tier 3: Few Students
Tier 2: Some Students
Tier 1: All Students

Tier 1: All Students
- District 96 Language Arts curriculum
- District 96 Math curriculum
- Academic Extension / Academic Intervention (AE/AI)

Tier 2: Some Students
- Study Skills class
- After School Assistance Program (ASAP) for Reading, Writing, and Math
- Evidence-based instructional programs in Reading and Math for identified specific skill deficits

Tier 3: Few Students
- Evidence-based instructional programs in Reading and Math for identified specific skill deficits (with increased time and intensity)

Tier 4: Special Education
- Special Education evaluation
- If found eligible:
  - Special Education Resource
  - Instructional curriculum in Reading, Writing, and/or Math

What is an Intervention?

An intervention exists as an opportunity for a student to receive the extra time and support he or she needs in order to demonstrate content, concept, and skill acquisition relative to the District 96 Curriculum and Framework. Interventions exist within District 96 as part of students' regular school day.

Our student are provided access to academic intervention on an individual basis, demonstrated through performance and assessment. The frequency and intensity of the support is determined by the individual needs of learners. As student need increases, so too does the frequency and/or intensity of support. Student progress is monitored regularly. As a student demonstrates proficiency regarding the targeted area of intervention, he or she will be cycled out of the specific intervention.

Practical

To be practical, a pyramid of intervention must be affordable given the school's available resources (time, space, staff, and materials). Intervention plans don't need to cost a lot. Instead, teams need to first think about how to use or reorganize existing resources to fully utilize what is already available.

At Woodlawn and Twin Groves Middle Schools in Kildeer Countryside CCSD, a 30-minute intervention block is built into the middle of the school day. The intervention block represents dedicated and protected time that guarantees students access to more instructional time and support. Teams decide which students will participate in which interventions at the beginning of each week based on formative assessment data. The intervention block is scheduled so that students do not miss direct instruction. By offering a block of dedicated and protected time during the regular school day—a sacred time during which interventions are available to all—students who have been identified by name and need are provided the kind of targeted support they need to be successful.

Effective

To be effective, the pyramid of intervention needs to be accessible, available, and operational early enough in the school year to make a difference for students. Teachers in a PLC reject the traditional notion that schools wait for a student to fail before intervening. Intervention plans should have flexible entrance and exit criteria designed to be responsive to the needs of students.

DuFour, DuFour, Eaker, and Karhanek (2004) define the goal of an effective pyramid of interventions as providing time and support as needed until

> students demonstrate they are ready to assume greater responsibility for their learning. The focus is on gradually weaning the student from the extra time and support as the student becomes successful in classes. The interventions then serve as a safety net if the student should falter, but they are not intended to be a permanent crutch. (p. 167)

This goal is possible only when the faculty has developed clear criteria that move students from one level of the pyramid to another until the student eventually demonstrates mastery.

Essential

To be essential, the pyramid of intervention must focus on the essential outcomes of the district's curriculum and be targeted toward a student's

TAKE AWAYS

Effective Interventions
1
2
3

specific needs. Using data, teachers regroup students based on the identified outcomes to provide the appropriate intervention. For example, at Kildeer Countryside Elementary School, the math lab provides target-aligned support to help students master specific skills using a prescription sheet completed collaboratively by the teachers on the students' grade-level teams.

After discussing the results of formative assessments, teachers are better able to provide targeted time and support. According to Guskey (2010), effective interventions possess three essential characteristics: (1) They present concepts differently, (2) they engage students differently, and (3) they provide students with successful experiences. It is critical that teacher teams identify essential standards and analyze assessment data together in order to purposefully plan and target their instruction.

Directive

To be effective, intervention is mandatory—not invitational—and a part of the student's regular school day. At Willow Grove Kindergarten and Early Childhood Center, teachers use the very beginning of each school day to deliver targeted interventions to specific students. Meanwhile, the rest of the students focus on "welcome work" that extends and reinforces their learning. Students are not able to opt out, and parents and teachers cannot waive students' participation in the intervention programs. Learning is not optional. School leaders must remain resolute in their responsibility to respond when students don't learn.

Time is one of a school's biggest resources, and the daily schedule represents an opportunity to maximize the impact of interventions. In many schools, the daily schedule has evolved over time and contains more untouchables than anything else. The reasons why the schedule is the way it is have long been forgotten, yet the schedule is often overlooked as a potential leverage point. In fact, creatively using time is one of the biggest leverage points available to principals seeking to improve their schools.

In their seminars, Rick and Becky DuFour frequently suggest that principals consider three questions when thinking about the schedules at their schools: First, do we believe it is the purpose of our school to ensure all students learn to high levels? Second, do we acknowledge that students learn at different rates with differing levels of support? Third, have we created a schedule that guarantees students will receive additional opportunities to learn through extra time and support in a systematic way, regardless of who their teachers might be? If the answer to these questions is "yes," the schedule can be reorganized to create time during the day when every available person becomes a contributing member of the support offered as part of the pyramid of interventions.

Providing students with additional time and support does not require more time or an extended day, but it may require a reallocation or realignment of existing time to guarantee regularly scheduled time for interventions. Schools that are committed to the idea that all students can learn will ensure that students will be able to access the pyramid of intervention as often as needed, daily or even multiple times during the day if necessary.

In addition to schoolwide, systematic pyramids of intervention, schools also may institute procedures that ensure student progress is checked on a regular basis. In these schools, students do not fall through the cracks, because checking on student progress is embedded into the routine practices of the school. As an example, consider the impact instituting a 9:1 schedule had on the availability of time for enrichment, extension, *and* remediation.

As a condition of using this structure to provide more time and support for students, teachers are required to work collaboratively to set common learning targets and plan units of instruction over a 10-day (two-week) period. It also necessitates that teachers at each grade level adhere to a consistent daily schedule or time period when delivering instruction in the same content areas. In other words, all third-grade teachers are scheduled to teach reading at the same time during the day.

Using the 9:1 model, each teacher delivers direct instruction to his or her own students for the first nine days of the unit. While the instructional strategies may vary among teachers, the learning targets being addressed remain consistent. On the ninth day, each student takes the same CFA (a short quiz or common formative assessment) covering the targets that have been taught over the past two weeks.

The 10th day is designated as a flex day in which differentiated intervention is delivered to all the students in all of the classes in a grade level. During their team meeting, teachers for this grade discuss the results of the assessment and regroup the students based upon how well each individual student has demonstrated mastery of the learning targets.

The 9:1 schedule is an effective strategy, because it ensures that no student falls through the cracks by guaranteeing that students will not go longer than three weeks without having their progress reviewed. It also has the advantage of providing a consistent opportunity for interventions during the regular school day. It is also efficient because it requires no additional time, staffing, or space to deliver differentiated time and support to students. Figure 5.5 shows graphically how the 9:1 model works.

On the flex day, some of the students will need reteaching or a dose of intensive remediation. Most students will demonstrate appropriate progress but will benefit from practicing with similar material. Other students will demonstrate mastery and be ready for enrichment activities related to the unit of study.

Figure 5.5   The 9:1 Intervention Model: Finding Time for Interventions

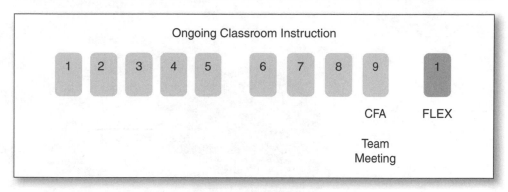

Staffing for the interventions is based on assessment results. The teacher whose students had the best overall performance on the assessment takes responsibility for working with the students who need more time and support to learn—those who have not *yet* demonstrated mastery of the material. Teachers may create smaller sections of the intervention group to isolate the skills in a more targeted way.

Other teachers work with students who are progressing but would benefit from further instruction or continued practice with a particular set of skills. This middle group usually has the largest number of students, and teachers may create multiple sections of this extension group to manage the numbers more efficiently. The team may also decide to utilize an aide or another certified member of the faculty in a team teaching approach.

The remaining students, made up of those who have demonstrated mastery of the standard, work with another teacher or certified member of the faculty on enrichment activities. In secondary settings, these students may function as peer tutors for other students. See Figure 5.6 for a visual representation of how students are distributed and interventions differentiated on the flex day.

The idea works equally well using a three-week schedule. Employing the same strategy, teachers plan and deliver a unit of instruction over a three-week period. On the 14th day, teachers administer, score, and analyze the results of an assessment. Again, the team meets to regroup the students and assign them into enrichment, extension, or intervention groups before providing them with differentiated instruction on the 15th day. An advantage of a 14:1 model is the alignment of the flex days with more formative assessments that are embedded in the unit of instruction. Figure 5.7 depicts the 14:1 intervention model.

The advantage of these types of models is that the teaching and student assignments are fluid; both will change every cycle based on the results of the assessments.

Figure 5.6   Distribution of Interventions on the Flex Day in a 9:1 Schedule

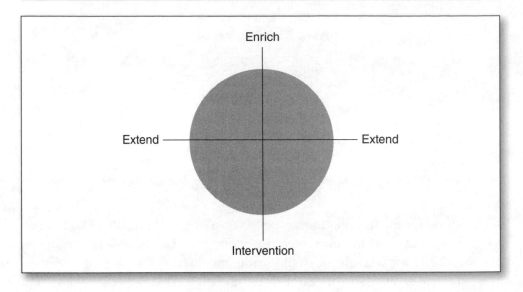

Figure 5.7   The 14:1 Intervention Model

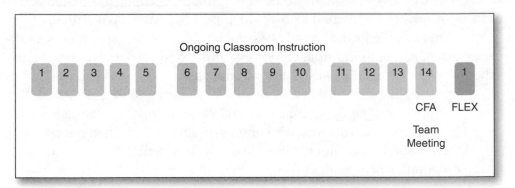

At the elementary level, assessing students in literacy (reading and writing) and numeracy (mathematics) can be managed by scheduling one flex day each week. The model in Figure 5.8 on the next page illustrates how using a three-week schedule cycles through a rotation of the major subjects and corresponding flex days. By organizing instruction in this way, time for regular reteaching and remediation is built into the schedule without overwhelming a faculty's resources. The flex days are rotated for each of the different content areas, as Figure 5.8 shows.

As DuFour, DuFour, Eaker, and Many have suggested, "It is disingenuous for any school to claim its purpose is to help all students learn at high levels and fail to create a system of interventions to give struggling

Figure 5.8 Rotating Flex Days on a Three-Week Schedule

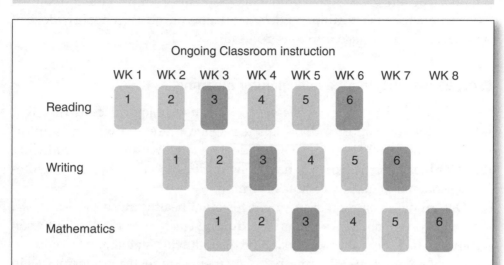

learners additional time and support for learning" (2006, p. 104). In schools committed to the belief that all kids can learn, principals take that message to heart and embrace the SPEED criteria to ensure their pyramids of intervention are on target and answer the question, "How does our school respond when students don't learn?"

THE SECRET TO SUCCESS

The secret to getting ahead is getting started. The secret to getting started is breaking your complex, overwhelming tasks into small, manageable tasks, and then starting on that first one.

—Mark Twain

Common assessments represent a powerful leverage point for principals seeking to improve their schools. When asked to describe the best place to start the journey toward becoming a PLC, DuFour explains that what he had come to realize was that one of the best strategies to promote the development of a PLC was to engage collaborative teams in the process of developing common assessments. He argues that "common, team developed, frequent and formative assessments are such a powerful tool in school improvement that no individual or team of teachers should be allowed to opt out of using them" (DuFour et al., 2006, p. 55).

Why is this? Perhaps it is because we learn best by doing. When principals ask teachers to develop common assessments, they provide the context for teachers to make meaning of their work and introduce a healthy dose of professional dissonance into the process.

Professional dissonance and making meaning

The concept of *cognitive dissonance* is a psychological construct that refers to the discomfort individuals feel when presented with new information or a different perspective that doesn't align with what they already know or believe to be true. We have long understood that the act of resolving dissonance actually promotes learning.

Designing a common assessment fosters a healthy dose of *professional dissonance* on collaborative teams by requiring teachers to work together on a common task. For a moment, examine the following statement: "Common, team-developed frequent formative assessments are such a powerful tool in school improvement that, once again, no team of teachers should be allowed to opt out of creating them" (DuFour et al., 2006, p. 55).

By definition, the content of a common assessment is the same for all members of a team who teach the same class, course, or grade level. The term used to describe the degree of consistency required on an assessment is not "sort of" or "kind-of" common. There are no "mostly" or "largely" common assessments. We don't hear people argue that the "bulk" or the "preponderance" of their common assessment is the same. There is no ambivalence—common means common.

The phrase *team developed* requires that everyone on the team be actively engaged in the design and development of the assessment. Some argue that delegating the responsibility of writing the common assessment to one member of the team or rotating responsibility and taking turns to write the assessment is an acceptable practice. Unfortunately, this is an example of shared practice, and the only person learning anything is the individual responsible for creating that unit's assessment. Instead, we would advocate that the entire team participate and work together to identify what learning targets will be assessed and even which items will and will not be included on the assessment.

Common assessments serve two purposes: to identify which students need more time and support and to identify which instructional practices were most effective in helping students learn. We do not advocate infrequent common assessment because of the importance of these two concepts. The requirement that the assessments be *frequent* causes teachers to routinely identify students that are and are not reaching proficient levels of learning. It also requires them to regularly consider feedback regarding the impact their teaching practices have on student learning.

Finally, the term *formative* refers to how teachers can best use the results of an assessment to guide decisions about teaching and learning. According to DuFour (2013), a summative assessment gives the student the chance to *prove* what he has learned. A formative assessment gives the student the chance to *improve* upon his learning. In a PLC, teams place an emphasis on using formative learning to improve teaching and learning.

Some might think it impractical to write common assessments before reaching consensus on what students are expected to learn. Others might argue that it is impossible to target interventions until teachers have evidence of what students did or did not learn. But, as teachers work to write a common assessment, they reconcile any differences between what all students should learn and what each of them has taught. Resolving that kind of dissonance among teachers is healthy. Rick DuFour explains,

> The questions of a learning community really flow up and down from collaboratively developed common formative assessments. We have found that people don't really start to think and act like a learning community until they are engaged in a collaborative effort to answer the question, "How do we know our students are learning?" (personal communication, July 30, 2005)

When agreeing on which targets should be included in a valid and reliable assessment, teachers begin articulating what all students will know and be able to do as a result of the class, the course, or the unit of instruction. Next, teachers must identify what was actually taught during the unit. The final step is to compare what was actually taught with what it was agreed that all students should learn.

The answers to the questions, "What should students learn?" and "What have teachers taught?" do not always align. Reconciling the professional dissonance caused by differences between what teachers agreed students should learn and what teachers actually taught enhances teachers' knowledge of both their content and pedagogy. In this way, working together to develop a common assessment promotes greater clarity around Question 1: What do we want students to know and be able to do?

Common assessments also provide a powerful and practical context for teachers to make meaning of their work. Even when agreement is reached on what all students should learn and be able to do, standards and learning targets remain abstract until they are translated into changes in classroom practice. In truth, teachers can return to their classrooms and teach what they have always taught, unless there is some concrete way to analyze the degree to which all students in the same class, course, or grade level were able to learn what was expected. As Sam Redding said, the task of creating common assessments provides "an operational definition of the standards in that they [the common assessments] define in measurable terms what teachers should teach and students should learn"(2006, p. 86).

As teams examine data from their common assessments, they inevitably discover that some students have learned and others have not. Once teachers gather data about who did and did not learn, the natural inclination is to reflect on their instruction and ask, "What do we do now?" Dialogue about ways to help students who are not learning—or who are already learning and are capable of learning even more—are powerful opportunities to promote more reflective practice. This collaborative dialogue promotes consideration of Questions 3 and 4 from the four critical questions introduced at the beginning of this chapter: What will do when students do or do not learn?

Implement PLCs by beginning with the design of common assessments. Engaging teachers in the use of common assessments provides a practical context for them to make meaning of their practice and requires the resolution of important questions. Using common assessments is a powerful way to promote the job-embedded professional learning that transforms schools. The secret to success is simple; begin the process of becoming a PLC by collaboratively developing common assessments.

6 Take Away the Training Wheels

Leverage a Collaborative Culture

The collaborative team is the engine that drives the PLC effort. Some organizations base their improvement strategies on efforts to enhance the knowledge and skills of individuals. Although individual growth is essential for organizational growth to take place, it does not guarantee organizational growth. Building a school's capacity to learn is a collective rather than an individual task.

—DuFour, DuFour, Eaker, & Karhanek (2004, p. 3)

Studies have shown that "when teachers are given the time and tools to collaborate, they become life-long learners, their instructional practice improves, and they are ultimately able to increase student achievement far beyond what any of them could accomplish alone" (Carroll, Fulton, & Doerr, 2005, p. 10). When teachers work together on collaborative teams, they improve their practice in two important ways. First, they sharpen their pedagogy by sharing specific instructional strategies for teaching more effectively. Second, they deepen their content knowledge by identifying the specific standards students must master. In other words, when teachers work together, they become better teachers.

Studies have also found that working on collaborative teams generated positive changes in teacher attitudes. Gallimore, Ermeling, Saunders, and Goldenberg (2009) noted teachers, those working on collaborative teams, were more likely to attribute gains in student achievement to improved instructional practice, rather than to external factors such as student traits or socioeconomic status. In contrast, teachers who did not work on collaborative teams had the opposite experience and tended to attribute achievement gains to factors outside of their control (Gallimore, et al., 2009).

What is also encouraging about Gallimore's study is the finding that collaboration had a significant effect on a teacher's sense of efficacy. As Thomas Carroll noted when reviewing Gallimore's research, "It is empowering for teachers to know that they can overcome external factors to increase student achievement when they use collaborative inquiry protocols to improve their instruction" (Carroll, et al., 2010, p. 71).

The MetLife Survey of the American Teacher reinforced Gallimore's findings and uncovered another important connection (Education Resources Information Center, 2009). Not only were teachers eager to team up with others in these new collaborative relationships, but those teachers who were very satisfied with their careers often worked in schools with highly Collaborative Cultures. For principals, the implications of the study were unmistakable; collaborating with others improved a teacher's sense of efficacy.

While collaborating with others improves a teacher's instructional practice, attitudes, and efficacy, research also shows that being a member of a high-performing collaborative team has a positive impact on students. According to Goddard, Goddard, and Tschannen-Moran, "The more teachers collaborate, the more they are able to converse knowledgably about theories, methods, and processes of teaching and learning, and thus improve their instruction" (2007, p. 879). In their study, they found "evidence of a positive and statistically significant relationship between teacher collaboration and student achievement" (Goddard et al., 2007 p. 891). Specifically, Goddard and his colleagues found that teacher collaboration had a statistically significant effect on student achievement on standardized math and science tests. They reported a one standard deviation increase in teacher collaboration "was associated with a .08 standard deviation increase in average school mathematics achievement and a .07 standard deviation increase in average school reading achievement" (Goddard et al., 2007, p. 890). Furthermore, Goddard and colleagues noted that these improvements occurred even when student characteristics such as race, gender, and socioeconomic status were taken into account. The researchers concluded their discussion by pointing out that

> at the very least, our results suggest that schools with greater levels of teacher collaboration did indeed have significantly higher levels of student achievement. Thus, not only is collaboration good for teachers-quite possibly by fostering teacher learning-but it is also positively related to student achievement. (Goddard, et al., 2007, pp. 892–893)

The question then is this: If collaborative teams improve teachers' practice *and* their students' achievement, shouldn't formation of such teams be one of the high-leverage strategies that principals employ to improve their schools? The most effective principals embrace this idea and design master schedules that provide designated and protected time for teams to meet during the regular school day. They support the creation of team norms and SMART (specific and strategic, measureable, attainable, results-oriented, and time-bound) goals targeted at improving student learning, design specific methods for monitoring the work of teams, and review all their policies, practices, and procedures in order to promote collaboration in their schools.

A ROSE BY ANY OTHER NAME: WHAT IS IMPORTANT ABOUT COLLABORATIVE TEAMS?

When visiting a school in the early stages of developing as a professional learning community (PLC), I heard the principal proudly exclaim, "Our PLC teams meet twice a month." He continued enthusiastically, "When our PLC teams are meeting on the second and fourth Tuesday of every month, our school is *totally* devoted to the idea that all kids can learn." I am confident that this principal did not intend his statement to spark my curiosity, but it made me wonder what his teachers are "totally devoted to" on days when they aren't meeting in PLC teams.

Paul Farmer, a national consultant on developing PLCs, observed that too many principals act as if relabeling teams as PLCs will miraculously make the teams more effective and efficient. The notion that simply placing a new label on a team meeting is somehow transformational misses the mark. Labeling teams with new names is *not* a high-leverage strategy. In fact, it may be one of the lowest leverage strategies principals can employ, if only because of the additional time and energy that goes into communicating, clarifying, and correcting exactly what this new team is supposed to do.

Honestly, we have never understood the rationale behind designating grade-level or departmental teams as PLCs. The truth is that teachers are members of all kinds of teams: grade-level teams, departmental teams, interdisciplinary teams, job-alike teams, child study teams, problem-solving teams, and a myriad of other teams. Simply adding "PLC" to the team name does nothing to improve a school. All it does is create another team!

When asked why he chose to designate these new team structures "PLC teams," this principal explained that labeling teams helped create greater clarity around purpose. In theory, this approach may sound like a good idea, but in practice, it can have the opposite effect. Creating new team structures inevitably generates questions such as "Who will be on the new team?" "When will these new teams meet?" and "What will the new team do?" All of these questions come from the teachers' legitimate desire to understand how the new team will affect their professional lives.

All of us seek to understand how change will impact our environment, and it takes time to articulate, clarify, reiterate, and respond to all of the queries. If questions and concerns are handled poorly, we create confusion, not clarity. Eventually, a debate will take place about whether an issue is appropriate for the PLC team or would be better suited for some other team. Teachers' attention shifts from *solving* the problem to *assigning* the problem to the proper team. Confusion and frustration inevitably follow, along with cynical observations like "See, PLCs don't work!"

Even with a new name, teams that remain focused on the same old, tired issues will not improve their school. As DuFour, DuFour, Eaker, and Many observed, "The pertinent question is not, 'Are teachers collaborating?' but rather, 'What are teachers collaborating about?'" (2006, p. 91). Creating new teams with new names puts the focus on the wrong thing. Instead, principals should concentrate on creating clarity about the right work existing teams should embrace.

It is far more efficient and effective to utilize existing team structures—ones that may already exist but may lack a clear purpose—and focus on why teams are beneficial, how successful teams function, and what tasks teams should engage in to help all children learn. Let's be clear; the reason some schools are more successful than others has nothing to do with the way they label their teams. Principals who want improve their school leverage the power of teams—regardless of what they are called—and focus on a few things that make a big difference. In PLCs, principals encourage teams to clarify the essential outcomes by class, course, or grade level; develop common assessments and establish proficiency targets; and analyze the results of common assessments to shape intervention programs and identify which instructional practices were most effective. Principals share evidence of effectiveness in the form of videos of efficacious teams in action, articles describing necessary practices at different stages of implementation, and artifacts illustrating what successful teams do when they are meeting.

For example, the faculty at Legacy High School (a large, suburban high school in Broomfield, Colorado) uses a graphic organizer to explain what teams are expected to do when they meet. Legacy High School's graphic organizer serves as a tool to communicate what is important and reminds faculty, "This is what we agreed to work on during collaborative team time." The one-page document describes tasks—things like creating common course assessments, articulating common course outcomes and essential learning, agreeing on team SMART goals, and determining common grading practices—that teams routinely engage in during team meetings. Behavioral expectations—such as "participate in unfiltered, constructive dialogue," "commit to and follow through on decisions," and "focus on identified areas of weakness for improvement"—are also incorporated into the document. Teams at Legacy High School use the graphic organizer to build on norms that describe how they will work together.

With his familiar words, "A rose by any other name would smell as sweet," Shakespeare reminds us that what something *is*—not what it is called—is what really matters most. To improve their schools, principals should worry less about what a team is called and more about what a team does during their meetings. Instead of creating another team, labeling it a "PLC," and waiting for something magical to happen, principals should help existing teams identify and improve the practices that will help all children learn.

THE ELEPHANT IN THE ROOM: MAKING TIME FOR COLLABORATION

> A principal who was implementing the PLC model in her school explained that their biggest challenge was dealing with time. "Every time we meet as a faculty, we wrestle with how to find more time. It is the elephant in the room and the one thing that is preventing us from really becoming a PLC."

Principals often ask, "How will we find the time to collaborate?" The answer is that we won't *find* the time. The reality is that we already have all the time we are ever going to have, and if principals want more time for teachers to collaborate, they must *make* time by changing the daily schedule and routine of their school.

Nearly 25 years ago, Schlechty observed, "The one commodity teachers and administrators say they do not have enough of, even more than money, is time: time to teach, time to converse, time to think, time to plan, time to talk, even time to go to the restroom or have a cup of coffee. Time is indeed precious in school" (1990, p. 73). In a PLC, a teacher's experience shifts from working in isolation to working in collaboration with others. As teachers' experience changes, so must the way teachers use time.

You will never find time for anything. If you want time, you must make it.

—Charles Bruxton

Finding time for teams to meet can be one of the most perplexing problems principals face when implementing the PLC model. But on this point, the consensus is clear; one of the critical conditions for the development of Collaborative Cultures is *designated, protected time* for teachers to meet during the regular school day. As Raywid says, "Collaborative time for teachers to undertake and sustain school improvement may be more important than equipment, facilities, or even staff development" (1993, p. 30).

Creating designated and protected time for teams to meet during the regular school day is a high-leverage strategy for principals who want to promote the development of a Collaborative Culture in their schools. There is no closet in which schools store extra time or secret desk drawer holding a stash of reflective moments. Because we are never going to *find* more time, we have to *make* more time for collaboration if we want to ensure that teams are successful. The daily schedule is an especially powerful leverage point when changes are made that will provide teams with regular, designated, and protected time to meet.

Long ago, principals acknowledged that there is never enough time for everything we want to accomplish, but according to Louis, Kruse, and Marks as reported by Reimer, "The principal plays a critical role in the development of professional learning communities, forging the conditions that give rise to the growth of professional learning communities in schools" (2010, p. 3). Providing time for teams to meet during the regular school day is one of the conditions necessary to the success of collaborative teams.

Principals can create more Collaborative Cultures by changing the structure of the day and making collaboration a priority. Watts and Castle (1992) have identified five strategies principals can use to make more time for collaboration:

1. *Free up time.* Creating more time for teachers to collaborate can be accomplished by freeing up some of the teachers' time spent on routine duties. The existing daily schedule does not change; instead, teachers are temporarily relieved from regular duties to collaborate on special projects or at designated times during the school year. To accomplish this, another teacher, an administrator, an instructional aide, or even a volunteer covers a teacher's responsibilities.

The benefit of this strategy is that it does not disrupt the existing routines of a school. The disadvantages are that this approach is typically only a temporary solution and is not systematic or schoolwide. Freeing up time in this manner does little to ensure a long-term commitment to creating a more Collaborative Culture in a school.

2. *Purchase time.* A second strategy for making time available is simply to purchase more time for collaboration. Schools often release teachers through substitutes or pay for summer writing projects. Some schools have found success by paying teachers to attend Saturday work sessions. One caution is that this approach removes teachers from the classroom, and teachers often struggle with the idea of being away from their students. Furthermore, while some teachers welcome an opportunity to work together in the summer or on a Saturday, many others have busy personal schedules and other commitments that conflict with Saturday or summer work schedules.

Purchasing time can be a fiscal challenge, but purchasing time for collaboration can work so long as there are funds to support the practice. This strategy can be used for ad hoc committees, onetime events, or specific projects, but purchasing time on an occasional basis does not promote long-term solutions to the challenge of providing more time for collaboration.

3. *Restructure or reschedule time.* It can be complicated to reschedule or restructure time, but doing so yields lasting changes that are more comprehensive and systematic. Common strategies for this approach involve banking time or scheduling late arrival or early release days that alter the traditional calendar, school day, and/or teaching schedule.

Restructured or rescheduled time has some obvious advantages over purchasing time, but there are problems nonetheless. The disadvantage of this approach is that students are typically not on campus or in session during the restructured or rescheduled time, which conflicts with community expectations that students be in school. Thus, creating time for teachers to work together while students are not on campus creates a public relations challenge for the building principal; communicating with the community about the rationale for such a change is an additional burden that must be considered when using this time-making strategy.

4. *Make better use of existing time.* In an effort to identify ways to better use time, some schools are conducting time studies and asking teachers to track how they use the time that already exists in their school day. For example, making better use of time allows faculty meetings to shift from forums for long and exhausting verbal memos to more opportunities for real and reflective collaboration among teachers. As teachers move through the various stages of PLC implementation, the use of time shifts.

Teachers find they benefit from spending less time learning about the work and more time working on the work.

This approach to making more time for collaboration can have a lasting impact on the culture of a school. As teachers examine the current reality of the way time is used, they confront a host of issues related to the school's mission, vision, values, and goals. How time is used in school says a lot about a school's purpose and priorities.

5. *Schedule common planning time.* Common planning time is designated and protected time for teachers to work with their colleagues. The idea of planning time is not new, but the creation of common planning time typically requires changes to the daily schedule. Schools can arrange schedules in three ways: according to tradition (adult centered), to facilitate instruction (teaching centered), or to facilitate collaboration (learning centered). The question for principals is, "Why is the schedule the way it is?"

In some schools, the schedule has not changed in years. Further examination often shows that unchanging schedules are based on unspoken norms such as the most senior teacher gets the last hour free or the teacher with the longest morning commute always has first period open in case he or she encounters traffic delays. These schedules are organized around adult convenience and almost never generate more time for collaboration.

Likewise, schedules can be arranged in ways that facilitate the logistics of instruction. For example, an art teacher may demand that all the first-grade classrooms be scheduled consecutively, or a PE teacher may request that PE classes in the same grade level be scheduled back-to-back, so the equipment and materials do not have to be exchanged between periods. A schedule organized in this way places a high priority on the logistics of teaching but does little to promote more time for meaningful collaboration.

Alternately, a schedule may be designed such that all teachers from the same class, course, or grade level are available to meet at the same time. Common planning time, as a strategy to create more time for teachers, works best when teachers from the same grade level or department meet with the clear intention to use the planning time for collaboration. In these schools, time for collaboration—in direct support of student learning—is the most important consideration when building a schedule.

Many principals realize that establishing a Collaborative Culture is a high-leverage strategy they can use to improve their schools. Looking at how time is used and designing a master schedule that includes time for collaborative teams to meet during the regular school day is a leverage point principals can use to promote the development of a collaborative culture.

THE TURNING POINT:
BUILDING COLLECTIVE CAPACITY

ca.pac.i.ty /kə'pæsɪti/—a noun meaning maximum productivity

Capacity building is defined as: actions that lead to an increase in the collective power of a group to improve student achievement, especially by raising the bar and closing the gap for all students.

—Fullan, 2005, p. 4

Another leverage point principals can use to improve their schools is to intentionally build the capacity of teams to function in a culture driven by inquiry, growth, and continuous improvement. Engaging in specific actions designed to build the collaboration capacity of teachers is a high-leverage strategy for two reasons.

First, building capacity is a reflective process that promotes better teaching by more teachers more of the time. As principals promote experiences that increase the collective capacity of the faculty, knowledge about the most effective ways of improving teaching and learning becomes more available and accessible to all teachers on a daily basis. Second, the process of building capacity is a shared experience; the experience of collaboratively building a faculty's collective capacity promotes greater commitment. The most effective principals understand that conversations about improving teaching and learning are more powerful when they take place within the context of a teacher's own school.

School improvement is most surely and thoroughly achieved when teachers engage in frequent, continuous and increasingly concrete and precise talk about teaching practice.

—Fullan, 2007, p. 97

It is gratifying to see teachers who know *what* they are doing. However, it is far more gratifying to see teachers who are able to articulate *why* they are doing *what* they are doing. In the most successful schools, teachers not only talk about what they do; they are able to articulate why they do it.

For the most effective teachers, the "why" is something more than intuition, opinion, or a preference based on past practices. They rely on their best professional judgment and choose whether to employ a particular instructional strategy based on their understanding of the research coupled with evidence gathered from their own experience. Teachers in schools with high levels of collective capacity find that reflecting on their practice is an ongoing, regular, and valued part of their daily routine.

As Fullan observed, "When schools establish professional learning communities, teachers constantly search for new ways of making improvements" (2008, p. 16). The goal of individuals striving to build the collective capacity of their school must be a culture where teachers work together to plan, teach, reflect, and apply new insights to their daily work. This never-ending journey in search for new ways of improving teaching and learning requires commitment. Unfortunately, the simple act of providing time for teachers to reflect on their practice is not as common as one might think. The first place principals should look to build collective capacity is the master schedule. As mentioned earlier, they should ask themselves, "Does our school provide designated and protected time for teacher teams to meet during the regular school day?"

Building the collective capacity of a faculty is also a shared experience, but schools are not very good at sharing what works and what does not. On one hand, Fullan says,

> There is a strong body of evidence that indicates teachers are the preferred source of ideas for other teachers. On the other hand, the evidence is equally strong that opportunities for teachers to interact with one another are limited, and that when good ideas do get initiated by one or more teachers, the support of other teachers is required if the ideas are to go anywhere. (2007, p. 75)

Fullan's observation creates a quandary. If we believe creating opportunities that allow teachers to learn from one another will result in higher levels of collective capacity, and we believe that teachers truly benefit from opportunities to share but are rarely allowed to engage in them, how are principals and teacher leaders to respond? One answer is to create more formal opportunities for teachers to exchange ideas and build the collective capacity of their school.

The power of collective capacity is that it enables ordinary people to accomplish extraordinary things.

—Fullan, 2010, p. 72

Principals can use four proven approaches that create formal opportunities to build the collective capacity of their school. All four—visioning retreats, reflective audits, sister school exchanges, and learning fairs—are effective strategies for facilitating nearly any change, but each is especially powerful when the goal is building the collective capacity of a school.

Visioning retreats

In Kildeer Countryside Community Consolidated School District 96, teams of teacher leaders representing each school in the district were invited to a one-day retreat at the end of the year. The one-day "Chautauqua" was designed to build capacity and promote continuous improvement. Teams had time to celebrate what had been accomplished and identify what needed to change to improve the school.

The Chautauqua became an important leverage point for principals. Participation by teacher leaders promoted the development of a shared vision, reinforced the school's Collaborative Culture, and became a place for staff to come together and celebrate. It also served as a place for principals and teachers to learn together. All of these practices built the capacity of teams to engage in collective inquiry and continuous improvement.

Reflective audits

Interchangeably called progress reports, appraisals, or reviews, the process begins by gathering teachers' perceptions and collecting artifacts to support their description of their school's current reality. Examples of artifacts include such things as lesson plans, common assessments, team meeting agendas and minutes, and samples of student work. Sometimes, principals assume that a particular practice is more deeply embedded than it really is, but when gathering work products and producing a portfolio of artifacts, a faculty is more aware of the current reality in their school.

The audit concludes when an external team of teachers and administrators is invited to review the data, examine the artifacts, and ask the faculty a series of probing questions that correspond with what is known to be best practice. The dialogue between peers around specific problems of practice forces teachers to reflect in ways they may not have considered before.

Sister school exchange

A sister school exchange is another way principals can build capacity. This idea involves teams of teachers visiting each other's schools to learn more about how other teachers have incorporated effective teaching practices into their daily routines. Participants share their own successes while "expanding their repertoire of strategies through exposure to practices effective at other school sites" (Meyers, 2012, p. 93).

During a sister school exchange, teachers readily identify common concerns that are present in their schools. The process of publicly reflecting on their practice builds the collective capacity of the faculty and allows teachers to articulate their best hopes and worst fears while focusing on the next steps to improve their school.

Learning fairs

A final leverage point principals can use to build capacity is a learning fair. The purpose of a learning fair is to promote reflection and celebration of what was accomplished during the previous school year. Much like a science fair, each school prepares to report on an important aspect of their work during the previous year. By reflecting on their professional practice through visioning retreats, reflective audits, sister school exchanges, and learning fairs, teachers and schools that have made only halting progress can begin to see remarkable results.

> *The skinny is that nothing succeeds like collective capacity.*
>
> —Fullan, 2009, p. 41

For many faculties, building the collective capacity of teachers can be the turning point in schools seeking to maximize their productivity. One of the most effective ways to build collective capacity is to provide teachers with formal opportunities to reflect and celebrate. In fact, intentionally creating opportunities to build collective capacity is such a powerful leverage point for principals that it should be recognized as a required component of every principal's annual school improvement process.

PACKAGE COURIERS, METER READERS, AND COPIER REPAIRMEN: LEVERAGING OPPORTUNITIES TO SHARE BEST PRACTICES

Scott Thurm recounts a conversation he had with a package delivery courier in the elevator of a large, multistory building in downtown San Francisco. He asked the courier if it was "more efficient to start at the top of the building and work down, or start at the bottom of the building and work up?" to which the courier replied, "It depends on the time of day." (Thurm, 2006, p. B1)

The courier had learned some useful information about the elevator patterns of the office building. That knowledge—unique to his particular assignment—was learned through repeated attempts to be more effective and efficient. Thurm wondered, "What would happen when the courier changed routes? Would the next courier have the same knowledge about the elevators? If not, how long would it take to learn the same information? Would the productivity of the package delivery company decline until his successor learned the same lessons?"

Thurm (2006) recounts another story about inspectors who read water meters in London. Managers had sought to improve efficiency by giving the inspectors handheld computers and allowing them to take their trucks home, thus eliminating the need to gather each morning at a central dispatch office. The expectation was that the new system would save time and increase efficiency. However, it turned out the dispatch office was far more than a place for the inspectors to change clothes and pick up their trucks. The dispatch office was actually a place for colleagues to share information and learn vital tricks of the trade. As Thurm explained, "The need of the inspectors to meet and share their ideas was so great that they began to meet on their own at a local restaurant: jotting down tips, solutions, and new ideas in a notebook they stashed behind the lunch counter" (2006, p. B1) to be referenced at a later date.

Finally, Thurm (2006) describes how a major company was attempting to increase the efficiency of the technicians who repaired copiers. Despite the fact that the company supported each technician with intensive training and a detailed reference manual, the technicians found they relied more on practical tips gleaned from talking with one another about solutions. The expected increase in productivity did not materialize until the company began using handheld radios to allow the technicians to confer with each other when they worked on repair jobs. Through conversation, technicians were able to benefit from the collective experience of others.

According to Sergiovanni, "Learning Communities have faith in the craft knowledge and wisdom of those closest to the classroom" (2005, p. 131). Just as it was important for the package courier, the meter readers, and the copier repairmen to share what they had learned, there is also "a pressing need for the nation's teachers to transform their personal knowledge into a collectively built, widely shared, and cohesive professional knowledge base to meet the needs of the next generation" (Chokshi & Fernandez, 2005, p. 6).

Thurm's stories of the package courier, the meter readers, and the copier repairman provide the context for one of the most challenging problems in a PLC—how principals encourage the collaborative sharing of craft knowledge between and among teachers. Like the package courier who found ways to manage the office building elevators to make his work productive and efficient, individual teachers learn from each lesson, and successful principals understand they cannot afford to leave the sharing of that craft knowledge to chance.

In the best schools, teachers learn from one another, yet most schools aren't structured in ways that allow experienced teachers to pass their craft knowledge to beginning teachers. Likewise, there are few mechanisms for beginning teachers to share new and innovative ideas with their veteran colleagues. Like the package courier, meter readers, and copier repairmen, many teachers struggle with finding opportunities to share their craft knowledge in meaningful ways. The most effective principals set aside time for teachers to meet, help teams clarify their priorities, and reduce isolation by creating a culture committed to collective inquiry.

Even with all this in place, however, teachers may not behave as teams. In traditional schools, most teachers are left to determine the effectiveness of their practice alone, in isolation, and by themselves. In too many schools, teachers are left to draw conclusions regarding the effectiveness of their instructional practices without feedback, perspective, or validation from others. When at least one hour each week is set aside during the regular school day specifically for collaborative planning, principals help build the capacity of teachers to share and exchange ideas about improving their pedagogy.

Mike Schmoker believes principals can leverage the work of teams by making systematic use "of simple tools that promote both alignment and collaboration" (2002, p. 6). For example, Schmoker (2002) suggests a monthly show-and-tell strategy—for as little as an hour a month—as an easy way to encourage teachers to share what they have learned about teaching and learning. Schmoker's position is simple and straight forward: "The use of disarmingly simple tools can be the difference between unfocused and highly productive teams" (2006, p. 106).

As mentioned before, a great place to look for leverage is within the time allocated for traditional faculty meetings. By canceling or limiting the number of faculty meetings, principals can dramatically increase the amount of time available for teachers to work in collaborative teams. Principals who are not comfortable with the idea of eliminating the faculty meetings may be encouraged to know that many principals have been successful by moving away from typical format of traditional faculty meetings. Instead of hosting the kind of gatherings that bear a remarkable resemblance to verbal memos, principals model the kind of collaborative conversations that encourage teachers to share their experiences.

A leverage point can be as simple as finding a timely article or chapter on a specific problem or question, designing a process for learning, and helping staff apply it to their experiences and context. A powerful leverage point for principals is the creation of formal and informal opportunities for teachers to engage in the intentional sharing of their practice and find ways to meet, share, and collectively build on their craft knowledge together.

TAKE AWAY THE TRAINING WHEELS: THE DIFFERENCE BETWEEN MONITORING AND MICROMANAGING TEAMS

Have you ever felt you had created the structures for collaboration in your school? That you had provided teams with the time and tools to collaborate, had defined the work, and checked for consensus every step of the way? Have you ever felt you had done all the right things to ensure teams would flourish in your school, and yet the teams simply weren't producing kinds of results you had expected? It is not uncommon to create the structure necessary for successful teams only to see it slip away during implementation.

It is a low-leverage strategy to assume that the presence of the right structures alone will be enough to ensure teams are successful. Creating schedules that set aside designated and protected time, encouraging the use of consensus-building processes, and requiring that teams create norms and write SMART goals are all essential steps to creating collaborative teams. Yet, principals must do more. We have found that ensuring teams are successful also depends on the specific actions principals take to monitor the work of teams.

In most organizations, what gets monitored gets done. In a PLC, monitoring begins by ensuring that every teacher regularly addresses and responds to the critical questions of learning as a member of a collaborative team. These questions (What do we want our students to know and be able to do? How will we know they have learned it? What will we do when they do or don't learn it?) are the centerpiece of the work that takes place around the table of every team meeting.

How effectively each team answers these critical questions becomes one of the principal's primary monitoring responsibilities and an excellent leverage point. The best way for principals to fulfill this responsibility is to have firsthand knowledge of what teams are doing on a daily or weekly basis. This requires regular communication between the principal and collaborative teams. To accomplish this, principals create systems that allow them to monitor the teams in their schools without micromanaging them.

Principals in the most effective schools promote collaboration by embracing a concept described in the literature as *directed autonomy*. According to Richard DuFour, principals who promote a culture of directed autonomy "foster autonomy and creativity (loose) within a systematic framework that stipulates clear, non-discretionary priorities and parameters (tight)" (2007, p. 39).

A culture of directed autonomy is at the core of highly effective, self-directed collaborative teams, but principals approach the task of promoting this idea in different ways. Some embrace the belief that regularly attending team meetings is the best way to manage teams. Those who choose this approach do so based upon the belief that close, constant supervision of teams is the key to improved performance. Others recognize the practical limitations of the principalship and focus on building the capacity of teams.

The most effective principals believe that skillful teams are successful teams. Instead of routinely attending every team meeting, they concentrate on monitoring the artifacts and products generated by teams during the natural course of working on the right work. It may seem counterintuitive, but attending every team meeting is one of the least effective ways to promote a culture of directed autonomy. Rather than encouraging growth, this practice smothers teams and contributes to the illusion that, because the principal is attending the meeting, teams are being monitored effectively. This is simply not the case.

There are a number of reasons why routinely attending every team meeting is a low-leverage strategy. Principals who opt for this strategy must understand that, no matter how well intentioned it is, the constant presence of the principal at every team meeting will eventually cripple the collaborative culture in their schools. Teams will never reach their full potential until principals remove the training wheels that come along with the constant presence of the principal, assistant principal, or coach in team meetings. They must trust that given the right level of time and support, teams will accomplish what needs to be done. Here are five reasons principals should not make a habit of regularly and routinely attending every team meeting.

Reason 1: The tone and the tenor of the team meeting are never the same

Let's be honest. The moment a principal sits down, the tone and the tenor of the team meeting change. It is no longer "a meeting with the team," but "a meeting with the principal." Despite the principal's efforts to stay in the role of an impartial and interested observer, the team inevitably defers to the principal who, like it or not, becomes the de facto leader of the meeting. Principals should not attend every team meeting unless they are willing to become team leader of every team in the building; at that point, why not simply hold a traditional faculty meeting?

Reason 2: The responsibility shifts from the team to the principal

Having the principal present at every team meeting diminishes the responsibility a team feels for their decisions. Less responsibility means less commitment. If decisions don't produce the intended results, the natural inclination is to shift responsibility for the lack of success. The conversation might go something like this: "It didn't go well, but the principal approved it, right? He was sitting right here when we made the decision, right? If it was a bad idea, he should have stopped us before we wasted our time."

Reason 3: No single individual possesses all the knowledge, experience, and expertise necessary to make meaningful contributions, suggestions, or recommendations regarding a team's instructional practices for every class, course, or grade level

Does it make sense, for example, to expect someone who trained to become a high school mathematics teacher and spent her entire teaching career at the secondary level, and who now serves as an elementary school principal, to provide meaningful suggestions regarding teaching emergent readers at the kindergarten level? No, it is unreasonable to expect a principal to be an expert in every subject, at every grade level. Time and again, teachers have reported that the best ideas about how to improve teaching and learning come from other teachers. Principals can and should support structures that allow teachers to meet and plan for effective instructional lessons, but to assume that having the principal attend every team meeting will somehow contribute to that goal is both irrational and illogical.

Reason 4: It is the wrong response to the problem(s)

Principals who feel they must attend team meetings to ensure teachers may actually meet are really focusing on accountability or responding to resistors. What these leaders fail to understand is that, while teachers will attend the meeting because they are compelled to do so, they will be attending out of compliance. Those resistant to the idea of collaboration before will not embrace collaboration simply because the principal is sitting in the room. By being present, a principal may increase attendance but fail to address the root cause of the problem. A more appropriate response would be to confront the individual who is not engaged and seek—or, if necessary, require—more professional behavior.

Reason 5: It is an inefficient use of a principal's time and talent

When attending meetings consumes the daily schedule, there is simply not enough time to attend to all the other tasks that fill a principal's to-do list. More important, this one-size-fits-all approach ignores the fact that some teams need little support, while others might benefit from extensive involvement by the principal. It is an illusion to believe treating every team in the same way will provide the level of differentiation teams need to be successful. If the standard is that the principal will attend every meeting—whether the team needs him or her—the schedule may very well prevent principals from attending those team meetings where help is truly needed.

When asked to articulate a rationale that supports the practice of regularly and routinely attending every team meeting, principals offer myriad reasons. None of them justify the continued use of this inefficient and ineffective practice. A far better way to promote a collaborative culture of directed autonomy is to focus resources on building the capacity of teams to do the work. The truth is that teachers learn to be collaborative by collaborating.

Principals who feel they must attend team meetings so that teachers will stay focused and productive may actually be reflecting a lack of confidence in their teachers to function as collaborative teams. An effective way to respond to this fear is to train team leaders in ways to organize and run a good meeting—it just makes sense that principals can foster more productive team meetings by training teams to be better teams. Giving team leaders the tools and strategies to design and deliver effective and efficient meetings ensures that teams will be productive now and in the future.

Principals improve how teams function when they provide professional development around important structures like norms and protocols, team roles and responsibilities, and agendas and goal setting. They can also assist teams by modeling practices in faculty meetings that can be replicated in team meetings. Simply put, principals can do far more to help teams develop a collaborative culture by providing them with the right tools and training than they could ever hope to accomplish by attending every team meeting.

Perhaps the best way to promote a collaborative culture is to monitor the work products of the teams. If teams are responding to the critical questions of learning, they will naturally generate products that demonstrate and document the topics they are discussing, the goals they are pursuing, and the outcomes they have achieved.

High-performing schools are interdependent self-directed collaborative teams, and a culture of directed autonomy is critical to their development. Effective principals realize that instead of micromanaging teams by attending every meeting and monitoring what teams do every step along the way, they would be better served to spend the same amount of time and energy training team leaders and monitoring the products teams generate in the process of collaborating about teaching and learning.

Alternatives to micromanaging collaborative teams

One of the most effective and efficient ways principals can monitor teams is to be visible and available. Dropping into team meetings from time to time is a powerful leverage point for principals. During these informal and impromptu visits, principals look for evidence of teams using pacing guides, analyzing common assessments, planning for interventions, and sharing strategies for delivering more effective lessons. Principals watch for collaborative behaviors and focus their attention on how time is spent during team meetings.

Encouraging reflection and self-assessment is also a powerful tool through which principals can monitor teams. Several excellent rubrics describing various stages of team development are available; two that come to mind immediately—one published in *Building a Professional Learning Community at Work: A Guide to the First Year* (Graham & Ferriter, 2010) and another in *Learning By Doing* (DuFour et al., 2006)—provide principals with concrete blueprints for monitoring the development of teams. Allowing teachers to reflect on the progress of their teams not only keeps them focused on developing their own expertise but also provides opportunities for the principal to monitor the progress of teams through the eyes of the team members themselves.

Principals can also monitor teams by asking specific questions designed to gather evidence that teams are focused on the right work. In Kildeer Countryside CCSD, teams bring results of their assessments to regularly scheduled meetings with their principal. In these meetings, principals ask three important questions: (1) Which students are proficient? (2) Which students are not proficient? (3) How is the team providing more time and support for the students who are not yet proficient? The questions not only serve as a way to monitor teams but also allow principals to engage in discussions about teaching and learning, gain firsthand knowledge of student progress, and help teams reallocate and match resources to help students learn.

A prerequisite of effective monitoring is regular and systematic communication between the principal and the teams in their schools. Teams have found countless ways to share information with principals, and many routinely share minutes of team meetings on a weekly basis. Some teams use handwritten journals for this purpose, while others have incorporated technology, using e-mail and podcasts as the vehicle for communicating between collaborative teams and the principal. Teams at the aforementioned Legacy High School in Broomfield, Colorado, use specially designed electronic templates to report progress and keep absent team members in the loop. The templates also serve as an archival record of the team's work.

Another very effective way to monitor teams is through the routine review of a team's work products. Many schools have found that that creating TUFF (Teachers United For Focus) notebooks facilitates the collection of artifacts. Each TUFF notebook contains, the team's SMART goal(s) for the year; copies of team's norms, meeting agendas, and minutes; and examples of any work products the team has generated in response to the critical questions of learning. The TUFF notebook is kept in a central place, so it is always available for review by the principal and members of the team. Teachers in Allen Parrish, Louisiana, found that TUFF notebooks were a very effective way to keep focused on student learning while simultaneously informing their principal of the results of team meetings.

Finally, some schools have adopted the use of specific tools designed to structure team meetings and agendas. In *The Collaborative Teacher* (Erkens et al., 2008, p. 35), a graphic organizer is described as one such tool. The organizer has places for teams to record their SMART goal, team norms, purpose and nonpurpose for the meetings, and an outline of the team's past work. The organizer also includes a section titled "Next Steps." Teams are encouraged to end each meeting by describing (in writing) what was accomplished and what they plan to discuss at the next team meeting. At the very bottom of the planning form, there is space for teams to identify an area of concern, request specific training, or simply ask a question of their principal. Once the organizer is forwarded to the principal, this simple tool establishes the vehicle principals and teams use to communicate.

Establishing the monitoring of teams as a priority

We often hear talk about the importance of teams, but "a critical step in moving an organization from rhetoric to reality is to establish the indicators of progress to be monitored, the process for monitoring them, and the means for sharing the results throughout the organization" (DuFour et al., 2006, p. 27).

There are many ways to monitor the work of teams, but what all effective principals have in common is that they focus on monitoring each team's results. Instead of allowing teams to drift off course, principals keep their teams on the right path by routinely monitoring the work of teams in systematic ways.

Although it may seem that the work of an educator is solitary, no educator works alone. The work of analyzing data and making adjustments to instruction is necessarily a collaborative endeavor. In the course of a single day or single lesson, teachers are required to take action and make decisions that require the initiative of an individual. Good classroom teaching requires the ability to adjust and the capacity for spontaneity, improvisation, and good judgment. But, all our efforts—for better or worse—are mediated by the efforts of our colleagues. Schools cannot achieve their full potential without engaging in the creation of a Collaborative Culture.

Creating a Collaborative Culture is an intentional practice and critical to our success. DuFour, DuFour, Eaker, and Many describe collaboration as "a systematic process in which teachers work together interdependently in order to *impact* their classroom practice in ways that will lead to better results for their students, for their team, and for their school" (2010, p. 12). What we have learned is that improving schools is inevitably a communal challenge best addressed while working with others. By breaking down the walls of isolation, we can create new ways of teaching and learning together.

Creating a Collaborative Culture is an important high-leverage strategy for principals. Leaders look for opportunities to promote teamwork every day and do not assume that collaborative relationships will develop without guidance and direction. They continuously search for leverage points to build capacity and provide time, structure, and support to collaborative teams.

7 Reports From the Precinct Captains

Leverage a Results Orientation

When Mike Schmoker (2006) describes the components of a Results Orientation, he acknowledges the role that compiling, analyzing, and using assessment data plays in schools, but looking at data is only part of the story. An authentic Results Orientation goes far beyond the numbers. In truth, the only time collecting data at the building and classroom level can be justified is when it directly links to, and is an integral part of, efforts to improve teaching and learning.

Data represent a means to an end, not the end itself. When using data in a Professional Learning Community (PLC), the singular focus of building principals and classroom teachers should be on finding better ways to help students learn. In schools with an authentic Results Orientation, teachers engage in a host of reflective processes that improve their instructional practice and ultimately help all students learn. We offer three leverage points principals can use right now to develop a more robust and authentic Results Orientation in their schools.

> *When leadership is focused on results, on urging a formal, frequent review of instruction, teaching improves.*
>
> —Schmoker, 2006, p. 126

An efficient and effective way to promote a Results Orientation is to conduct quarterly reviews of teaching and learning at the classroom level. As envisioned, these quarterly reviews include the results of common assessments, but they go beyond looking at test data to identify the standards teachers taught during the previous quarter, the standards that have yet to be addressed, and the instructional practices teachers will use to ensure that their students will become proficient.

It is a bit tongue in cheek, but true: Students have a difficult time learning content that has not been taught. So along with results of common assessments, teachers should also be able to provide evidence (1) that they have taught the standards, (2) that students have been given the opportunity to learn what the team agreed was important for all students to know and be able to do, and (3) that students were given additional opportunities to learn if they did not learn the first time they were taught. If principals want to foster a Results Orientation in their schools, they should institute a process to regularly review of the results of teaching and learning—one that goes beyond the test scores.

Schmoker (2006) encourages principals to get out of their offices, onto the teaching floor, and into classrooms in order to foster a genuine Results Orientation. He recommends that, in addition to looking at the products of the lesson, principals look at grade books, team lesson logs, and unit plans. He argues that the focus should be on actual samples and artifacts of the work; the real outcomes of the teaching and learning process.

Another leverage point occurs when principals observe teachers during the evaluation cycle. Principals can shift the emphasis of the traditional teacher evaluation process from teaching to learning by focusing less on what the teacher is teaching and more on what the students are learning. Instead of concentrating on documenting the teaching behaviors, principals seek evidence to demonstrate the level of rigor of the lesson, or the extent to which students are engaged, or that learning is taking place. Dennis Sparks (2005) advocates that principals take note of the products students are generating as a result of instruction and require teachers to bring samples of student work to the postobservation conference. This way, the teacher and principal can assess the effectiveness of the lesson based on results. Leveraging this simple shift of a principal's time and attention during teacher observations creates a much stronger focus on results.

Finally, to create an authentic Results Orientation, principals should celebrate the results they want to see replicated in their schools. They should look for opportunities to identify, publicize, and praise behaviors that contribute to improved teaching and learning. As Evans said, "The single best, low cost, high leverage way to improve performance, morale, and the climate for change is to dramatically increase the levels of meaningful recognition for and among educators" (1996, p. 254).

Mike Schmoker observed that in establishing a results-oriented culture at Stevenson High School, "DuFour did one thing with passion and strict regularity: he made occasions to reward, recognize, and celebrate accomplishments at every single faculty meeting and more formally at the end of each semester" (2006, p. 146). Celebrating results is a powerful lever-age point principals can use to promote effective teaching practices and increase the probability that short-term modifications in teachers' behavior will become long-term transformations in the school's culture.

THE RIGHT INTERPRETATION OF A RESULTS ORIENTATION

In a school with the proper understanding of a Results Orientation, the focus is not on *gathering* data; it is on *using* data. Too often, data collected at the building and classroom level are funneled into dashboards and onto scorecards to justify thick school improvement plans generated by elabo-rate strategic planning initiatives or by requirements to generate volumi-nous documentation—neither of which has any significant support in the literature as a strategy that helps improve teaching and learning.

The appropriate use of data is an important part of building an authentic Results Orientation, and schools with the right interpretation of a Results Orientation use data to improve teaching and learning. In these schools, principals are careful not to put too much emphasis on the numbers alone—they realize a Results Orientation is much more. They do not burden their teachers with the responsibility of collecting or reporting assessment data to demonstrate alignment with district goals. Instead, they insist teachers use data to drive their instructional decision making.

In fact, compiling team- and classroom-level data for dashboards and scorecards is a low-leverage strategy. Every minute principals spend in the office compiling data for a dashboard or scorecard is one less minute they are in classrooms or with teacher teams engaged in the collective effort to improve teaching and learning. If the purpose of teachers' and principals' analysis of data is not explicitly and directly connected to the improvement of student learning, it is a tragic waste of their precious time and energy.

Scrutinizing more numbers doesn't make for a better Results Orientation; it just makes for a more time-consuming and complicated one. Compiling data and developing scorecards, dashboards, or portfolios that may be suitable for presentation at an upcoming Rotary Club meeting—or even to the board of education—is not the responsibility of teachers. The appropriate focus of teachers must be on using data to inform and improve their practice.

THREE RULES FOR USING DATA

Damon Lopez, former principal of Los Penasquitos Elementary School in San Diego, maintained that in order for teachers to maximize the impact of data generated by common assessments, principals should honor three rules and ensure that data are (1) easily accessible (timely), (2) purpose-fully arranged, and (3) publicly discussed. The principal is best equipped to create the necessary structures associated with the first two rules. Teachers, who are in the best position to talk about the implications of assessment results on their practice, must commit to the last.

Rather than having teachers work independently to turn data into information, successful principals find it far more productive to create the con-ditions under which teacher teams can make meaning of the data. Creating the conditions that support the successful application of the three data rules is a powerful leverage point to promote an authentic Results Orientation.

Rule 1: Accessible and timely data

Chapter 3's story describing the impact timely, accessible data had on the electrical usage of individual homeowners should not be lost on those striving to improve their schools. The point of that story is that when mean-ingful data are easily accessible, individuals are more likely to use that information to change behavior. The same is true for teachers and princi-pals. If the expectation is that data from common assessments will be used to inform or change practice, they need to be easily accessible to teachers.

For data to add value to a school's collective efforts to improve student learning, teachers' access to the data must be timely. In addition to figuring out who needs to know what by when, the key question for principals to ask is, "What is the most efficient way to return assessment data back to teachers?" To improve the timeliness and accessibility of data, principals need to shorten the turnaround time it takes to return data to teacher teams.

Data lose their impact whenever results take more than 48 hours to return to teachers. As Kim Marshall suggests, "When turnaround time after interim assessments is long, the results are stale and outdated by the time teachers sit down to discuss them" (2008, p. 65). Outdated information makes it more difficult for teachers to adjust instruction, identify students who need more time and support, and coordinate delivery of remedial or enrichment programs among members of the team.

Rule 2: Purposefully arranged

The second rule for maximizing the effective and efficient use of data calls for the results of common assessments to be purposefully arranged. Data delivered to teacher teams need to be presented in a format that is complete, accurate, and straightforward.

Data should be organized in simple—not simplistic—ways. There are many software packages that almost instantaneously arrange assess-ment results in tables, charts, or graphs that make it easy for teachers to digest. Author D. M. Griffiths illustrated why this is so important when he said, "If the message the information is trying to communicate fails to get through to the reader, [the information] is useless. It's better to be simple and understood than complex and ignored" (2006, p. 18).

What is important for principals to consider is how the data can be returned to teachers in simple, straightforward formats that are conducive to discussion. From time to time, teachers may create their own tables or graphs or request different formats for organizing assessment results. However, initially the data should be arranged in a format that allows teachers to focus on the data itself, not the *presentation* of the data.

Rule 3: Publicly discussed

Facilitating teachers' use of data from common assessments is a powerful leverage point for principals seeking to promote a Results Orientation. In fact, a case can now be made that using data generated by common assessments offers one of the most effective ways for principals to improve student learning. However, student achievement data are relevant only if the results are used to identify (1) which students have not yet mastered what was expected and will need additional time and support to be successful and (2) which teaching practices the collaborative team should retain, which they should refine, and which they should replace with other, more promising practices.

Each time teachers engage in the discussion of an assessment, they benefit from the collective wisdom of their team. By reviewing results as a team, teachers not only gain multilayered insights into how their students are learning but also get a better understanding of content knowledge and instructional pedagogy. Without a meaningful context, it is impossible for teachers to align results of their teaching with what is best—or even better—practice.

While principals are responsible for addressing the logistics of making data easily accessible and purposefully arranged, collaborative teams are uniquely equipped to engage in the collective and public discussion of what the data mean in terms of teaching and learning. Nothing justifies the giving of an interim assessment—or the associated loss of instructional time—unless teachers discuss the results of the assessment and adjust their instruction accordingly.

Of the three, Rule 3, Publicly Discussed, is the most important, and there is growing support for the use of protocols to accomplish this task. The increased acceptance of protocols has paralleled the growing consensus supporting the importance of high-performing collaborative teams. Many principals have found the regular use of protocols increases the effectiveness of team meetings. Likewise, many teachers have recognized the positive impact protocols have on their practice. Both principals and teachers have embraced protocols, because the effective use of protocols ultimately promotes higher levels of productivity.

PROTOCOLS: A POWERFUL PRESCRIPTION FOR PROFESSIONAL LEARNING

While protocols vary in significant ways, they all do two things: provide a structure for conversation—a series of steps that a group follows in a fixed order—and specify the roles different people in the group will play.

—Larner, 2007, p. 104

In their simplest form, protocols are a set of agreed-upon guidelines for a conversation. A protocol typically describes a specific—almost prescriptive—process that structures the work of teams. The description of a protocol outlines such details as the purpose, expected outcomes, step-by-step directions, number of participants, roles of team members, and time requirements. According to Lois Brown Easton (2009), there are four categories of protocols: looking at student work, looking at professional practice, looking at issues and concerns, and looking at professional reading. All can positively impact the productivity of collaborative teams.

Looking at student work

As teams grow more skilled at using protocols, they become better students of their own students. This group of protocols places an appropriate emphasis on *using* data rather than *collecting* data. Teams that use these protocols to examine student work become faster and more accurate in the analysis of student data. Teachers using protocols are far more likely to look at student work collaboratively for the purpose of determining student needs than to look at student work in isolation for the purpose of assigning grades.

Looking at professional practice

As the use of protocols becomes more accepted, teachers begin to see the value of protocols as a tool to examine their professional practice. Instead of focusing on individual interests in team meetings, using protocols from this category helps focus conversations on the complex task of improving teaching and learning. The structure provided by these protocols keeps teachers engaged and on task, and establishes a precedent for collectively questioning current practice.

Looking at issues and concerns

Teams rely on this protocol category to help solve problems. Often teams get stuck and spend hours naming, renaming, and nicknaming problems. They identify and overidentify issues but lack the necessary skills to address them. They end up grinding away at their concerns with little success. This cycle of "find and grind" impacts a team's sense of collective efficacy in significant ways. Teachers quickly learn that protocols from this category provide teams with new, effective problem-solving tools.

Looking at professional reading

Finally, the regular use of these protocols fosters the development of more reflective practitioners. Sharing professional reading promotes a culture in which ideas are freely shared and strengths and weaknesses are openly explored. Using these protocols to facilitate discussion of articles allows teachers to thoroughly inspect challenging issues and think about the intended and unintended consequences of their actions.

The support for using protocols as a way to improve team meetings is compelling, but when principals first introduce the idea, they are often met with resistance. This was certainly the case in Kildeer Countryside Community Consolidated School District (CCSD) 96 in Buffalo Grove, Illinois, where principals found that a combination of top-down pressure (insisting that teams used protocols) and bottom-up support (providing additional training, effective facilitation, and modeling of protocols during faculty meetings) was necessary before teachers were willing to incorporate the regular use of protocols into team meetings.

> *Without an explicit structure, conversations about teaching and learning tend to drift, go in many directions at once, or become so abstract that they are unlikely to lead to any useful learning.*
>
> —Weinbaum et al., 2004, p. 47

Initially, some teachers felt protocols made conversations slow and superficial; they described their discussions as contrived and unnatural. Other teachers felt requiring teams to use protocols somehow limited their academic freedom or diminished their professional autonomy. In general, there was a belief that using a formal process to engage in structured conversations was nothing more than process for the sake of process.

Some of these concerns were true; using protocols did disrupt the communication patterns typically found in traditional team meetings.

This is because using protocols does not allow teams to engage in the kind of random, unfocused conversations many teams were accustomed to having. For some teachers, this shift to a more transparent, focused, and structured meeting format was uncomfortable and made them feel vulnerable. What principals came to understand was that the regular use of protocols promoted development of trust between and among team members. When teachers feel safe, they listen to each other more deeply. When combined with effective norms, protocols help teams navigate difficult conversations.

Other teachers found protocols challenging because of school cultures characterized by isolation and the privatization of their professional practice; early on, it became clear that the regular use of protocols challenged the mindless use of past practice as a precedent. However, protocols confronted the precedent in productive ways. Instead of enabling teachers to remain comfortable with the old, familiar way of doing things, protocols pushed teams to generate new alternatives. What had previously seemed impossible suddenly became possible. Principals and teachers had to acknowledge that no single individual had all the answers. With more knowledge and experience at the table, teachers were able to see possibilities and opportunities they may not have seen before.

Protocols improved communication between and among teachers as well by promoting dialogue over discussion and debate. Rather than allow individuals to be verbally trampled by an overzealous teammate, protocols structured conversations in ways that ensured every voice was heard. Principals found that conversations shifted in the meetings and saw that teachers engaged in focused dialogue designed to promote the sharing of new ideas and strategies. In contrast, teams that did not incorporate protocols were forced to continue to tolerate random discussions and behaviors that sanctioned the hiding and hoarding of best practice. It became clear that protocols encouraged exploration and alternative thinking, which took more time. But by slowing down, teams generated better options, ideas, and potential solutions for the team to consider.

Principals also saw that the regular use of protocols promoted development of a culture of inquiry. This allowed teachers, working with others confronting similar problems, to engage in continuous and substantial learning about their practice in the settings where they spent their professional lives. These teachers were more likely to seek out honest, growth-oriented feedback to promote high levels of student learning. In contrast, on teams where teachers resisted using protocols, relationships tended to favor the kind of polite, superficial feedback that protects adult relationships.

Protocols are one of the most powerful processes people can engage in to promote professional learning.

—Easton, 2009, p. 16

The effort to incorporate protocols as a tool to improve the effectiveness of team meetings took time, but it was worth the effort. The change required patience and persistence, but principals and teachers found the benefits of using protocols far exceeded the challenges of implementing them. As Lois Brown Easton said, "Protocols are the ideal vehicle for holding the professional conversations that need to occur in PLCs—conversations that will lead to increased student achievement and motivation" (2009, p. 1)

IT'S NOT PIXIE DUST; IT'S PROTOCOL

Some people think creating a Results Orientation on a team is magic and that, somehow, just a sprinkling of pixie dust will produce the magic. It's not pixie dust; it is the thoughtful—even artful—use of well-thought-out, carefully implemented, and skillfully facilitated protocols that make a difference.

The skillful use of protocols helps ensure that conversations among teachers are efficient and effective. Stevi Quate, codirector of the Colorado Critical Friends Group, defines a protocol as a set of agreed-upon guidelines for a conversation. Although there are literally dozens of protocols, Quate notes that all of them create a structure that makes it safe for teachers to ask challenging questions of each other (2003, p. 6). The kinds of conversations Quate is referring to are necessary if principals expect teachers to engage successfully in the analysis of assessment data or the improvement of a lesson.

Specifically, the purposes of protocols are to promote the examination of student work or to reflect on a teacher's pedagogy. Some protocols facilitate the analysis of data, while others focus on the examination of a lesson. There are protocols that generate suggestions for setting goals with students and others that analyze the relationship among lessons, standards, and rubrics. Still, others enable teachers to collect data, make comparisons, and track student progress. Some protocols provide structure for delving deeply into the quality of a teacher's pedagogy to identify strategies for improving an assignment, project, or assessment.

Protocols help teams analyze data, including student work, more quickly (efficiently) and more accurately (effectively). In teams, teachers study students' work closely and collectively, because this enables them to learn if and how students are learning. In the process of grading the work, they gain insights about students' strengths and weaknesses, their mastery of and misconceptions around the content, their proximity to or distance from proficiency, their progress with respect to a defined standard, or their unique ways of thinking and working.

Teachers can also use students' work as a way to capture the efficacy of their own work. They can determine whether their current instructional strategies are appropriate for a students' level of understanding or match a student's cognitive, cultural, and contextual learning needs. Looking at student work creates a Results Orientation and provides the context for decision making.

When teachers meet to talk about student learning, they sharpen their pedagogy and deepen their content knowledge. According to the National Turning Points Center (NTPC; 2001), teachers who use protocols have a more comprehensive understanding of what students know and are able to do than teachers whose team discussions are not so structured. The regular use of protocols also helps teachers develop a shared language for assessing student work and a common understanding of what quality student work looks like.

Using protocols promotes a culture of continuous learning. David Allen (as cited in Weaver-Dunne, 2000) believes the process of looking at student work in a collaborative manner helps teachers take a closer look at how they teach. The NTPC (2001) believes protocols encourage collegial feedback and the critical analysis of student *and* teacher work in a safe and structured format. McDonald, Buchanan, and Sterling (2004) echo that belief and recommend using protocols because they foster cultures that do a better job of collaboratively assessing the quality and rigor of teachers' work.

Using protocols also builds a sense of community among and between teachers. NTPC (2001) argues that looking collaboratively at student work and participating in collective problem solving through the use of protocols moves teachers away from the isolating concept of *my students* and toward the community concept of *our students*.

Finally, use of protocols allows teacher teams to be more efficient. Quate (2003) reminds us that in most schools, time is the resource that is always in short supply. Once mastered, protocols become a valuable tool teachers use to focus collaborative conversations on what matters, thereby making the most of the time they do have.

Initially, many teachers may find protocols a waste of time and the examination of student work threatening. "Schools mired in norms of private practice and used to ignoring the actual impact of the practice on student learning may not take easily to learning with protocols," McDonald (2004, p. 1) observed. However, principals who encourage teachers to try them anyway find that even reluctant participants are attracted to them.

Teachers gain experience with using protocols, their confidence and comfort levels increase, and they recognize the benefits.

This is good news for teachers and principals seeking to create a Results Orientation in their schools. More enduring and practical than a sprinkling of elusive pixie dust, the use of protocols is a leverage point principals can use to promote positive and lasting results for teacher teams.

SOAP NOTES: A TOOL TO PROMOTE REFLECTIVE DIALOGUE ABOUT STUDENT LEARNING

SOAP noting is an example of a simple yet comprehensive technique to promote more reflective dialogue among teachers; it was first developed by the medical profession in the late 1960s. Doctors use SOAP notes to document a patient's symptoms, observations, assessments, and treatment plans. According to the American College of Sports Medicine, one of the major benefits of SOAP noting is that it organizes extremely complex problems into simpler tasks that are more easily tracked and solved (Durnstein & Moore, 2003, quoted in Ball & Murphy, 2008). The use of SOAP notes has also been shown to improve communication between those responsible for the well-being of a patient. Today, the practice of SOAP noting is used around the world by nurses, pharmacists, occupational and physical therapists, dieticians, social workers, psychiatrists, and physicians.

SOAP notes can provide similar benefits in schools. In education, much like in medicine, improving student learning is an extremely complex process involving many variables that can be difficult to track and resolve. Likewise, improving communication among teachers responsible for improving student learning will lead to higher levels of collaboration. Teams that adopt the SOAP noting technique as one of their primary methods of documenting and reflecting on assessment data can improve their communication, documentation, and planning for student learning.

Benefits of SOAP notes

SOAP notes are a data-driven process that emphasizes the natural progression from collection of relevant data to assessment of the learning problem to development of a plan of how to proceed. There are a number of benefits to regularly using SOAP notes.

The SOAP noting process provides teachers with a consistent method of compiling relevant information about how students are progressing through the curriculum. SOAP notes improve communication, help teachers identify obstacles, and provide a structure for developing plans to assist students in achieving their goals. SOAP noting also provides an efficient, standardized method for reflecting on student progress that is simple, concise, and compatible with data from common assessments.

SOAP notes provide teachers with a tool for managing the progress of all students, not just those in special populations. Teachers can customize their SOAP notes and use them as a way to track interventions or any factor that directly or indirectly impacts student learning.

Finally, SOAP notes capture concrete evidence of progress that teachers can share with other teachers, administrators, parents, and students. These notes provide a longitudinal record of teachers' collective efforts to improve student learning.

How do you write a SOAP note?

SOAP stands for **S**ubjective, **O**bjective, **A**ssessment, **P**lan. The written comments within a SOAP note can vary from teacher to teacher, but the general principle remains the same: to record the progress of the student(s).

Subjective: **Subjective description of student progress as reported by the teacher**

This first section of the SOAP note calls for teachers to describe the progress students are making based on their observation of students. The most common mistake teachers make in this section is moving from description to judgment (student was too tired to test well) or adding irrelevant information (room was too hot during testing period.)

An example of what teachers write in the Subjective section might be "Based on what I see when I check for understanding using the whiteboards, most of the students understand the concept of adding fractions with like denominators. A handful of students are still struggling, but overall, it would appear that the majority of students are proficient in adding fractions with like denominators."

Objective: **Objective account of the student's performance based on data**

Teacher judgment is usually accurate, but information in this section should be objective and contain limited analysis and/or judgment. When done well, the Objective section is data driven, provides a measurable description of the students' progress, and aligns with the teacher's Subjective observations. The most common mistakes teachers make in this section are being too global and failing to provide enough detail to define the learning issues students are experiencing.

For the Objective section a teacher might write, "In my class, 25 of 32 students scored 80% or higher on the last common assessment, which tested their understanding of adding fractions with like denominators. All seven nonproficient students scored less than 50% on the assessment. Three of the seven students who were not proficient did not show their work and made basic arithmetic mistakes when adding the numerators. The remaining four students who did not demonstrate mastery added the numerator to the denominator."

Assessment: **Teacher's understanding of the students' needs**

For this section, the teacher combines the subjective description as observed in the classroom with the objective data gathered from a common assessment and consolidates them into a short, concise, and factual appraisal of the situation. The most common mistake teachers make here is being too vague when describing the evidence upon which their appraisal of needs is based.

As an example for this section, a teacher might write, "With the exception of the seven students who were not proficient, the class is ready to move on to adding fractions with unlike denominators."

Plan: **Plan that ensures all students master the learning target**

This section can include specific interventions, homework assignments, or plans for using a new approach or teaching technique. When writing this section, teachers should ask themselves, "To enable my students to reach mastery, what do I want to do?" or "What do I want to cover with them next week?" The most common mistake teachers make in this section is failing to be specific when describing the recommended interventions. For example, writing "the student should continue to practice adding fractions" would not be sufficient.

An example of what teachers write in this section of the SOAP note might look something like this: "The three students who had difficulty with addition would probably have gotten the correct answer had they shown their work and reviewed it before turning in the assessment. These students will redo the problems they missed while verbally explaining the steps taken to solve the problem. The remaining four who were not proficient will review the algorithm for adding fractions with like denominators using manipulatives. After reviewing and relearning the concept of adding fractions with like denominators, each nonproficient student will be given an opportunity to take an alternate form of the assessment."

SOAP notes are not meant to be as detailed as a progress report, and they should fit on a single page. The length of a SOAP note will differ from teacher to teacher, but a short, precise SOAP note is always preferred over one that is too long. Abbreviations and partial sentences are acceptable, assuming they are understood and can be easily interpreted by other members of the faculty and staff. In the beginning, SOAP notes may be a little longer, but they typically become more concise as teachers gain more experience with the technique.

A well-written SOAP note tells a story

When done well, the SOAP notes technique is a simple way to promote an authentic Results Orientation by reflecting on student progress. SOAP notes improve communication, encourage the appropriate use of data, and document our collective efforts to help all students learn to high levels.

REPORTS FROM THE PRECINCT CAPTAINS

Historically, the school district, like most school districts, was addicted to formal rules and procedures and subject to an occupational culture that had proven itself to be particularly resistant to change.

Sound familiar? Perhaps, but if one substitutes the words *police department* for *school district*, you have a quote describing the New York Police Department (NYPD) during the mid-1990s. At that time, New York City was considered one of the most dangerous cities in America. Just 10 years later, New York was considered one of the safest. What triggered this amazing turnaround? What helped New York move from being one of the deadliest big cities in American to being one of the safest? The answer lies in a Results Orientation that relentlessly focused on the achievement of organizational goals.

The NYPD responded to the rising crime rate by instituting a practice that required precinct captains to publicly report the most current data on crime in their precincts and indicate how they were planning to improve on the current situation. The reports, using data benchmarked against internal and external sources, were delivered publicly in front of peers who shared a responsibility to ask clarifying questions, make suggestions, or add information from their own experience. The goal of these public meetings was not to find fault or place blame. It was to identify policies, practices, and procedures that would reduce the crime rate.

The strategy worked. From 2000 to 2001, New York City showed a 12.01% decline in major crimes (murder, rape, robbery, felony assault, burglary, and grand larceny). The two-year trend showed an 18.88 % decline in major crimes, and the eight-year trend showed an amazing 63.17% decline in major crimes (O'Connell, 2001).

A similar story can be told regarding student achievement in Kildeer CCSD. Since 1999, student achievement has steadily improved to the point where, today, more than 96% of all students meet or exceed state standards. Such a pattern of sustained improvement over an extended period of time is based, in part, on a strategy very similar to the one used in the NYPD. Structures were created that made the regular use of data and the sharing of best practices a routine part of the district's results-oriented culture.

APPLYING A RESULTS ORIENTATION IN SCHOOLS

Like the NYPD, the Kildeer district recognized that data needed to be gathered and analyzed in a timely manner if changes in instructional strategies were to be successful. And, like the precinct captains in the NYPD, principals were invited to attend periodic meetings were they were required to report and react to building-level achievement data.

During these data meetings, principals met with the superintendent, central office administrators, and the other building principals to discuss results of the most recent assessments. The goal of the meetings was to determine whether current instructional strategies were working to improve student learning. The foundation for the data meetings was built upon (1) access to timely data, (2) responsiveness to results, (3) use of effective teaching practices, and (4) relentless follow-through.

Within two weeks of the quarterly benchmark assessments, principals were expected to analyze the results and describe the current reality in their schools. They also prepared a description of what they planned to do to improve student learning and a timeline for implementation of their plans. Their proposed responses were scrutinized by colleagues and held against the standard of what was known to be best practice. Transparency was nonnegotiable; all appropriate data—reflecting both good and bad results—were openly shared. The focus of the meetings was on providing feedback and finding solutions. Everyone was expected to work together to find ways to improve student achievement.

TANGIBLE BENEFITS OF DATA MEETINGS

There were other benefits of data meetings. The school district found that institutionalizing this practice fostered the development of a more authentic Results Orientation. The meetings provided a context for the sharing of craft knowledge, promoted the development of new norms around best practice, and identified policies, practices, and procedures that needed to be changed in order to maximize student learning.

The data meetings emphasized collaboration and interdependent relationships. Principals were provided an opportunity to share their experience, the curriculum director was expected to offer suggestions for new teaching methods or training, and the business manager understood the rationale behind requests for funding. These results-oriented discussions between central office administrators and building principals developed into regularly scheduled meetings; *all* levels of the administration were required to attend, and all were expected to participate in a process to identify achievement trends, allocate resources, and assess the impact of various instructional strategies.

The data meetings also resulted in better communication among and between administrators. Not only did the data meetings improved *existing* lines of communication between and among administrators, but, perhaps more important, the meetings also created new ones. For example, for the first time in his career, the business manager sat in on discussions about instruction, and thus, he had a clearer understanding of the rationale behind requests for resources.

Communication improved in several other ways. First, the data meetings generated more frequent and focused communication within the school district about teaching and learning. The data meetings served as a regular reminder that learning—not teaching—was the fundamental purpose of the schools. Next, the data meetings facilitated more effective communication. While the district had used different reporting mechanisms to manage and monitor learning, the previous structures were the equivalent of "a series of one-way streets running parallel to on another. Today, thanks to [the data] meetings, communication channels have been converted to two-way streets—broad two-way highways with several lanes of traffic running in different directions at the same time" (O'Connell, 2001, p. 12).

Finally, the data meetings emphasized communication about the right things. The focus of the data meetings was on *results* and led to changes in instructional practice. The data were openly shared for the express purpose of collaboratively developing new and more effective strategies. By examining the relative performance of each school on the basis of the results of quarterly benchmark assessments—comparing each school to the others—the administrative team could determine efficiently and effectively whether or not an instructional strategy was succeeding.

A RESULTS-ORIENTED PRACTICE TRANSFORMS SCHOOL CULTURE

Perhaps the most significant feature of the quarterly data meetings was that data on student achievement were used, not just compiled. We have argued that too many departments, grade levels, or teams focus on the task of gathering data without a conscious effort to talk about what the data mean. Therein lies the main problem with the use of dashboards and scorecards at the classroom and the team level. Besides being time-consuming and complicated, these reporting mechanisms can and do shift the focus of teacher's time, energy, and attention away from *using* the data to the meaningless task of *compiling* the data.

By utilizing data generated by internal benchmark assessments and promoting open dialogue—even an occasional debate—about best practices, the data meetings transformed the school district into a learning organization that could adjust classroom pedagogy to align with best practice based on results.

Engagement precedes alignment and before teachers can align their teaching with best practice, they must engage in a process to understand what the data mean. All in the name of alignment, some systems-oriented practitioners have used the high-leverage strategy of a Results Orientation as an excuse to impose massive data-gathering expectations on principals and teachers—but that is the wrong focus. Indeed, engagement is a prerequisite of alignment, and teachers and principals need to embrace the critical importance of publicly discussing assessment results in order to create the context for any meaningful changes in their practice.

Section III

PLC Strategies

8 What's on Your Refrigerator Door?

Clear Away the Clutter to Clarify What's Important in Your School

When was the last time you looked—I mean really looked—at what's on the door of your kitchen refrigerator? My guess is that most refrigerator doors probably look a lot alike, scattered and busy with papers, pictures, and notes. Although you might characterize it as clutter, you can tell a lot about what is important to people simply by seeing what is on their refrigerator doors.

As a principal, you can extend the metaphor of the refrigerator door to what is important in your school. Obviously, we are not talking about the refrigerator door in the teacher's lounge; rather, think about using the metaphor to examine what is important in your school. For example, does a look at your school's metaphorical "refrigerator door" reveal that your school values learning or teaching? Working in isolation or on collaborative teams? Does your school tinker with every new idea that comes along or narrow the focus to a few strategies? What is it that *really* matters in your school?

Becoming a PLC is a high-leverage strategy, but it is not something a faculty engages in for a year or two, only to abandon before moving on to a new initiative. As Hargreaves observed, "Becoming a PLC [is a process that] creates an ethos that permeates a school" (as quoted in Sparks, 2004, p. 48). Principals recognize that becoming a Professional Learning Community (PLC) is part cultural, part structural, and not something that can be reduced to a recipe or a prescriptive set of activities. Becoming a PLC is not something you do; it is something you are.

Schools working to become PLCs are clear about what is important. Sometimes principals assume the PLC is more deeply embedded than it really is. By gathering work products and producing a portfolio of artifacts, principals can become more aware of the level of implementation of PLCs in their schools. Collecting examples or artifacts that support each of the three big ideas helps clarify and confirm a school's current reality. Examples of artifacts principals can collect as evidence of a Focus on Learning include a list of the essential outcomes for each grade level in—at a minimum—reading, writing, and math; team-developed curriculum pacing guides; and team-developed common assessments. Principals may also ask teachers for a description of how their teams are systematically providing time for intervention and enrichment.

They further their understanding of the current reality regarding the Collaborative Culture in their schools by collecting the norms and SMART (specific and strategic, measurable, attainable, results oriented, and time-bound) goals created by each team or gathering evidence about how teams are organized, when they are provided with time to meet, and how the work of the teams is monitored and supported.

Finally, principals can assess their schools' Results Orientation by collecting examples of how data generated by common assessments are presented to each teacher, by reviewing analysis sheets indicating team conclusions and strategies for improvement, and by analyzing and explaining how assessment data are used to identify which students—by name and need—would benefit from additional time and support and which teaching strategies were most effective in helping all students learn.

Focusing effort and energy on looking—*really* looking—at what your school values is worth doing. By first defining what is important (the three big ideas) and then clarifying your school's current reality through products and artifacts, you will be equipped to cut through confusing clutter on the refrigerator door and clearly answer the question of how your school is developing as a PLC.

A THOUSAND CONVERSATIONS: THE POWER OF CONSISTENT, CLEAR MESSAGES ABOUT WHAT MATTERS

The task of becoming a PLC requires that principals engage in a thousand individual conversations; each held one at a time.

—Mike McDonnell, personal communication, March 15, 2011

Becoming a PLC involves everyone in the process of change. If principals hope to create schools where all children learn to high levels, they must commit to engaging in constant, clear, and consistent communication about the big ideas of a PLC. Or, as Mike McDonnell, a principal in Thornton, Colorado reported, "The task of becoming a PLC requires that principals engage in a thousand individual conversations; each held one at a time" (personal communication, March 15, 2011).

The first key to communicating a vision is repetition. John Kotter (1996) estimates that leaders routinely *underestimate* how much communication is needed to facilitate change by a factor of 10. The reasons for this miscalculation are many, but failing to engage in constant and continuous communication of the vision is one of the most common mistakes principals make when beginning the process of becoming a PLC.

Principals who are intent upon transforming their schools will pay close attention to the advice of Rick DuFour and return to the big ideas of a PLC again and again with "boorish redundancy" (DuFour, personal communication, July 30, 2005). DuFour suggests principals look for frequent opportunities to talk about a Focus on Learning, a Collaborative Culture, and a Results Orientation. The most effective principals will use the formal structures of faculty meetings, daily bulletins, and postobservation conferences to reinforce the basic tenets of PLCs. They will also take advantage of informal opportunities to engage teachers in conversations about PLCs over lunch, in the hallways, and on the playground.

In today's classroom, the rapid pace of change is accelerating even more, and the sheer volume of information flowing to teachers can be overwhelming. With the staggering number of messages teachers must sort through on a daily basis, is it any wonder that articulating a vision once or twice is simply not enough? Consider the unintended consequences that failing to communicate frequently had on one school's vision for a new model of assessment.

The principal made a conscious decision to move from an assessment system based on proficiency to one based on growth. The new initiative required a number of changes, but everything was in place for the first quarter. Yet, when the new assessments were distributed, teachers were surprised, shocked, and even dismayed with the new format of the exams. Their frustration was directed at the principal, who was baffled by the amount of anger and angst.

Tension grew, and the principal became disillusioned by the teachers' lack of support for his vision of a new approach to assessment. He felt teachers had dismissed his efforts to communicate and blamed the faculty's frustration on a handful of negative resistors. However, when asked *how and when* the change in the focus and purpose of the assessments had been communicated to teachers, he identified two times: once in a single paragraph of the back-to-school letter, and a second time during his opening day faculty meeting.

In truth, teachers had not ignored the announcement. Instead, they were focused on day-to-day information associated with the beginning of the school year. The proposed change in assessment practice was an important and legitimate initiative designed to help teachers and students alike. However, the information about the change in assessment practice had been washed away in a torrent of information delivered during the opening of school. While it may have seemed repetitive, what this principal failed to understand was the importance of articulating the key components of the vision over and over and over again.

A second key to communicating is a clear and consistent message. Using big words in long sentences buried inside complex paragraphs does not promote effective communication. Instead, it hampers understanding and gets in the way. As Pfeffer and Sutton observed, "It is hard enough to explain what a complex idea means when you understand it and others don't. It is impossible when you use terms that sound impressive but you don't really understand what they mean" (2000, p. 52).

The overuse of complex language leads to confusion and is often a sign that the person communicating—either verbally or in writing—doesn't really understand what he or she is trying to say. As Bob Eaker is fond of saying, "Making everyday things complicated is commonplace. Making complicated things simple is genius" (personal communication, July 30, 2005). A simple but not simplistic message can be powerful, and this is never more important than when principals are trying to communicate a compelling vision of a PLC for their school.

Principals enhance the credibility and the consistency of their communication efforts when teachers see a match between the behaviors described in the vision and what is valued in their school. Consider the confusion a principal created when, after months of emphasizing the importance of formative assessment and discounting the usefulness of summative data, he insisted his faculty begin the new school year by spending hours and hours analyzing results from the previous year's end-of-year, state-mandated summative assessment.

Teachers had grudgingly moved away from their long-standing tradition of analyzing longitudinal trends using the state's summative assessment data during districtwide data days. Was it any wonder they became confused and frustrated with the mixed message sent by the principal? Modeling behaviors that are consistent with the vision complements the impact of a clear and concise message.

Articulating the big ideas of a PLC over and over and over again is critical to success. To paraphrase John Kotter (1996, p. 95), one conversation here, another conversation there, and the number of times teachers hear the vision really begin to add up. Principals must look for frequent opportunities to communicate the vision. Principals enhance communication by (1) keeping their message simple, consistent, and crystal clear and (2) modeling behaviors that align with the vision.

The image of the elevator ride is applicable here; principals need to craft a message that is concise, free from educational jargon, and to the point. If the message can't be conveyed during the length of time it takes to ride an elevator to the next floor, the message is either too long or too complex.

To summarize, it isn't easy, but those working to transform their schools will embrace McDonnell's practice of holding a thousand individual conversations with different teachers, in different settings, at different times. If they couple frequent opportunities to communicate with a clear, concise, and consistent message, principals can ensure that the vision of becoming a PLC becomes a reality.

FLYING KITES: UNDERSTANDING THE CONCEPT OF LOOSE/TIGHT LEADERSHIP

Critical attributes of highly effective principals include clarifying what is important and communicating with consistent clarity. Leaders of PLCs must also understand the concept of directed autonomy, or said another way, when to hold tight and when to loosen one's hold. In this regard, the role of a principal in a PLC is complex, and it can be compared to flying a kite:

Imagine a beautiful spring day. The blue sky is dotted with white puffy clouds drifting along the horizon. The eager kite flyer runs across the field, pulling along a fragile collection of sticks and tissue at the end of a string.

For a time, the kite bounces along the ground and shows no inclination of ever getting off the ground. Eventually, and after much effort, the kite flyer manages to lift the kite a few precious feet into the air, but danger suddenly looms. The kite seems to be determined to dive toward electrical lines and tangle itself in tree limbs.

It is a defining moment for the kite flyer. Will the dangers keep the kite from soaring skyward to attain its ultimate height? The kite flyer adjusts tension on the string to redirect the kite and catch a puff of wind that lifts it upward. As the kite floats aloft, the kite flyer loosens the tight control and lets the string play out, enjoying the wonder of the kite soaring higher and higher.

A school's journey toward becoming a PLC is similar to this. Teachers are asked to collaborate in what are often unfamiliar ways. Relationships on newly established teams can be fragile. It may seem that those involved simply "bounce along," showing no inclination to work together, meet common goals, and get the initiative "off the ground." Early efforts to get PLCs underway seem fraught with danger, setbacks, and obstacles to overcome. It is critical during this initial period of development that a principal understand when to retain tight control and when the success of the initiative depends upon loosening that control, giving the PLC a chance to take off and soar.

There are times when a principal must be direct, set clear objectives, establish specific timelines, and create expectations. In holding tight to the big ideas of a PLC, principals are allowing the PLC to "fill with the wind." Likewise, there are times when principals need to give faculty time to work and encourage them to make decisions about what students should learn, how common assessments are developed, and what interventions to put in place for students who don't learn. This is the time for the principal to loosen control and give the teachers more responsibility. It takes both understanding and a considerable amount of energy to get the idea of a PLC off the ground, and the right combination of loose and tight leadership is the key insight for principals.

Another way for principals to think about the concept of loose/tight leadership is to reflect on the "why" of a particular activity. If the answer to a question appears to be related to "why," then the issue is likely something for the principal to retain tight control in addressing. However, if the issue is better described by "how," then resolution of the problem likely falls within the responsibility of the collaborative teams. As Rick DuFour often says, the answer to "why" is found within the big ideas of PLCs.

The first big idea of a PLC is a Focus on Learning. A school is focused on learning when it is responding to the critical questions of learning. These three questions form the foundation of a school's improvement efforts: (1) What should students be able to know and do as a result of this class, course, or grade level? (2) How will we know if they have learned? and (3) What will we do if they are or are not successful? Creating a Focus on Learning is a high-leverage strategy.

Second, teachers and principals cannot ensure that all students receive their best efforts unless the adults in the school work together. Therefore, creating a Collaborative Culture built upon high-performing teams is a second high-leverage strategy. Once teachers are organized in logical ways that reflect their curricular expertise and teaching assignments, teams devote their time and attention to answering the critical questions of learning, *together.*

Third, each teacher, each team, the school, and the system in general assess the impact of their collective efforts on the basis of tangible results. The faculty and staff work to monitor and manage the teaching and learning process and commit to responding to data from multiple sources to provide evidence of student success. An authentic Results Orientation is a third high-leverage strategy.

Louis, Kruse, and Marks found that "principals in schools with strong Professional Learning Communities delegated authority, developed collaborative decision-making processes, and stepped back from being the central problem solver. Instead, they turned to the Professional Communities for critical decisions" (1996, p. 193). Author David Straus concurs, saying simply, "If you have built alignment on the important issues of vision, mission, values and strategies, you should be able to trust others to make good decisions" (2002, p. 152).

DuFour and Eaker describe the dynamic of loose/tight leadership by saying,

> On one hand and at the same time, while they are encouraging autonomy and discretion, principals must insist on adherence to certain tenets that are essential to the PLC concept and make it clear that teacher autonomy does not extend to disregarding those tenets. (in DuFour, DuFour, Eaker, & Karhanek, 2004, p. 146)

The *certain tenets* that DuFour and Eaker were referring to are the high-leverage strategies of a PLC that help all students learn.

The "why" questions are nonnegotiable; they represent high-leverage strategies in a PLC. In fact, it is the very presence of these big ideas that separates schools functioning as PLCs from traditional schools. When faced with questions related to these big ideas, principals are most effective when they consistently hold tight to "why" an activity is important while leaving responsibility for the "how" of implementation to collaborative teams.

Learning communities will not survive and thrive without the right kind of leadership from the building principal; work with dozens of schools has provided us with ample evidence that the principal's ability to master the concept of loose/tight around the significant high-leverage strategies goes a long way to providing the kind of leadership so necessary to success.

9 Reboot the Principalship

Strategies to Rekindle, Reignite, Reenergize Your School

> *We can create the most effective generation of leaders ever by redefining and simplifying leadership around the core concepts of professional learning communities.*
>
> —Schmoker (2006, p. 29)

Despite a leader's best efforts to communicate the vision with great clarity, not everyone in school will be willing to do what is necessary to help all students learn. When that happens, principals must be willing and able to work with resistors and confront toxic behaviors in their school.

Asked what he thought was the key to getting teachers to embrace the idea of becoming a Professional Learning Community (PLC), Tom Koenigsberger, a nationally recognized science teacher, replied, "People just need to get off their 'buts' and start doing something" (personal communication, July 30, 2005).

Koenigsberger wasn't encouraging physical activity with his statement but rather the need for teachers and administrators to stop making excuses and start making the kinds of changes that ensure all students will learn. He went on to elaborate and asked, "How many times have we heard people say they support Professional Learning Communities *but* they are too busy, *but* they don't have enough training, *but* they don't understand exactly what is expected?" These "yes, buts" represent the comments from people who rarely challenge the idea of becoming a PLC publicly but who are resistors, nonetheless" (personal communication, July 30, 2005).

The point is that for those teachers and administrators who struggle with the idea of becoming a PLC, there never will be enough trust, enough time, and—no matter how hard we try—enough training. Principals working to transform their schools understand what DuFour meant when he said, "People committed to becoming a PLC will find a way. People committed to the status quo will find an excuse" (personal communication, July 30, 2005). Understanding and responding to resistors is an ongoing task for principals.

GET OFF YOUR "BUTS": RESPONDING TO RESISTORS IN YOUR SCHOOL

Broadly defined, resistance is a fearful reaction to change (Valencia & Killion, 1988). In schools, resistance is a natural response to organizational change that has the potential to impact an individual teacher's practice (Friend & Cook, 1996). Kerry Patterson suggests that as individuals are asked to change their practice, they ask themselves two things (Patterson, Grenny, Maxfield, McMillan, & Switzer, 2005). First, is the proposed change worth the effort? Second, will I be successful with this change? Principals invite resistance when they leave those two questions unanswered. Resistance to change can manifest itself in many ways, and when a teacher's response is "Yeah, but . . . ," it's helpful for the principal to identify the reason for the resistance.

Jo Ellen Killion provides principals with a useful way to look at resistance in their schools (Valencia & Killion, 1988). She suggests teachers can be resistant if they are not convinced the change in practice is a good idea (lack of commitment), if they lack the necessary knowledge and skills to feel successful (lack of skills), or if they have a diminished sense of efficacy (lack of confidence) around the idea. Whether the reason for resistance is a lack of commitment, a lack of skills, or a lack of confidence, schools functioning as PLCs are uniquely prepared to help teachers be successful.

Responding to resistors

Principals can address teachers' lack of commitment by building shared knowledge. What is important at this stage "is that we first engage staff members in building shared knowledge of certain key assumptions and critical practices and then call upon them to act in accordance with that knowledge" (DuFour, DuFour, Eaker, & Many, 2006, p. 39).

It is important to know what you are doing, but it is more important to know *why* you are doing it. To implement the big ideas of PLCs successfully, teachers, working in collaborative teams, need time to "make meaning" of their practice. The best way to accomplish this is to provide time for teachers to reflect, discuss, consider, and eventually understand why they do what they do. Indeed, if PLCs are to succeed, a principal must consciously create opportunities for teachers to build shared knowledge.

When the staff lacks necessary knowledge and skills to be successful, a principal's charge is to provide specific learning opportunities. In the early stages of implementation, teachers call for more and more training, but principals need to be careful. If principals continue to provide *only* training, they risk getting stuck in the process (training) and never get to doing anything differently (results).

The most effective principals understand that this issue will not be resolved with a single workshop or training program. The knowledge and skills essential to a successful PLC develop through a reflective process. Michael Fullan reinforced this idea when he said,

> Capacity building is not just workshops and professional development. It is the daily habit of working together, and you can't learn this from a workshop or course. You need to learn it by doing it and having a mechanism for getting better at it on purpose." (2010, p. 74)

Clarifying teachers' practice through a reflective process is essential for an effective PLC. "One of the key moments occurred when our teachers moved from learning about the work to doing the work," noted Jeanne Spiller, staff development coordinator in Kildeer Countryside Community Consolidated School District 96" (personal communication, 2006.) At just the right moment, the emphasis of staff development in Spiller's district shifted from providing training to providing support in areas where teachers needed it the most. And one of the most powerful ways she found to support teachers was to give them time to work together during the school day.

Some resistors don't believe they *can* be successful in a PLC. Jonathon Kotter made this point eloquently:

> Employees will not make sacrifices, even if they are unhappy with the status quo, unless they believe that useful change is possible. Without credible communication, and a lot of it, the hearts and minds of the troops will never be captured. (1996, p. 9)

When there is a lack of confidence or a diminished sense of efficacy on the part of teachers, principals can use short-term SMART (strategic and specific, measurable, attainable, results oriented, and time-bound) goals and celebrate small victories. Setting, achieving, and celebrating short-term SMART goals can help convince teachers that becoming a PLC is worth the effort *and* that they can be successful.

Howard Gardner (2006) created another approach to dealing with resistors. In his framework, Gardner identified seven ways leaders can "actively and powerfully" help people—especially adults—change their minds. A leader could engage in one or all of these approaches when faced with an individual who was resistant and unwilling, or unable, to make a contribution to the organization:

1. Reason—Making logical arguments

2. Research—Presenting factual knowledge

3. Resonance—Connecting with an individual's emotional core

4. Representational Redescriptions—Using stories to convey the message

5. Resources and Rewards—Providing incentives for change

6. Real-World Events—Examining examples of success of similar people

7. Resistances—Challenging longstanding beliefs (Gardner, 2006, p. 14)

All of these approaches will work depending on the situation. It is not uncommon to see examples of each being used in schools every day. Resistors are most likely to change when principals use the first six items on Gardner's list in combination with one another. However, and when all else fails, principals must be willing to confront toxic and unproductive behaviors in their schools. A principal shared the following all too familiar story:

During a team meeting, a teacher complained about the newly adopted mathematics curriculum. Her negativity was loud, persistent, and constant until she announced, "All the research says this program is bad for kids and I won't teach it!" When the principal, who happened to be observing the meeting, asked where she had read this research report and if she would be willing to share her source, she became indignant and stormed out of the meeting. After a moment of stunned silence, the team continued with their meeting.

Unfortunately, the story this principal shared is not unusual. In too many schools, too many teachers are allowed to opt out of teaching the agreed-upon curriculum, to disregard the results of common formative assessments, or to ignore the needs of struggling students. Too many teachers are also forced to tolerate colleagues who arrive late for team meetings, come unprepared to work, or are passive aggressive or disrespectful.

Far too many schools still operate under the premise that it is better to "go along to get along." In these schools, good, caring, and dedicated teachers feel they have no one to turn to for help and simply quit trying. They give up and just accept that they have to live with the "crazies." Why, they ask, would I want to create an adversarial relationship with someone I will have to work with for the rest of the school year?

In these schools, teachers and principals simply shrug their shoulders and walk away rather than confront their colleagues about toxic behaviors. Therein lies the tragedy of this story. It takes only one bad actor to ruin the culture for everyone else, and yet, in schools with negative and ineffective cultures, no one—not even the principal—does much of anything about it. That is the bad news. The good news is that we only need to look in the mirror to find someone to address this issue.

The principal in this story realized that he needed to preserve the integrity of the collaborative teams. He also knew this was not the first time this teacher had behaved in this way. Up to now, the principal had systematically applied each of Gardner's first six approaches but had avoided a direct confrontation for fear that it might negatively affect relationships at school. At the same time, he realized that what had happened was unacceptable, but he struggled with how best to respond to the outburst that had taken place.

Confrontation can be difficult, but it need not be negative

It takes great courage to confront toxic behaviors, but effective principals understand and accept the importance—even the inevitability—of conflict. As DuFour said, "It is possible to be tough-minded and adamant about protecting purpose and priorities while also being tender with people" (DuFour et al., 2006, p. 230).

Principals in schools with healthy cultures are "relentlessly respectful" and never embarrass, belittle, or condemn individuals in public. At the same time, they are "respectfully relentless" around the cultural norms that support learning. When important cultural expectations are violated—or worse yet, sabotaged—principals accept their responsibility to confront and redirect the violators or saboteurs. In fact, "a defining moment has occurred [in a school] when a leader chooses to confront rather than avoid saboteurs" (DuFour et al., 2006, p. 239).

Fullan assures principals that it is ok to be assertive (2010, p. 68). DuFour and Marzano take Fullan's comment a step further and argue that "it is not only okay [for principals to be assertive]; it is imperative" (2011, p. 30). DuFour and Marzano were speaking specifically to the importance of principals being clear, direct, and explicit about "the goals that are to be achieved and a few critical conditions they expect to see in every school" (2011, p. 33.)

Of the goals and conditions DuFour and Marzano were contemplating, surely their list would include such things as a culture focused on learning, teachers contributing to the work of collaborative teams, delivering a guaranteed and viable curriculum, using common formative assessments to drive instruction, and creating schoolwide, systematic pyramids of intervention to provide more time and support for students. In effective schools, principals do not allow teachers to engage in behaviors or ignore practices that do not align with what we know is best for students.

Confronting toxic behaviors

The ability to confront unproductive behavior successfully is one of a principal's most important skills. Kerry Patterson (Patterson et al., 2005) characterizes confrontation as the act of personally holding individuals accountable or responsible for their actions. When confrontations are handled well, problems are resolved and relationships improve. When confrontations are avoided, problems linger, and the potential damage to a school's culture is enormous.

Our best hope is that principals will recognize the importance of confrontation and keep working to get it right. Paraphrased from the book *Crucial Confrontations* by Patterson et al. (2005; used with permission), the following strategy helps principals successfully deal with confrontation.

1. *Choose What and If:* Clearly identify what is to be addressed, and stay focused on the behavior(s) when confronting the individual. Consider the implications that confronting or not confronting the behavior will have on your school.

2. *Master My Stories:* Illustrate the impact that the negative behavior(s) has on others, on the culture, and ultimately on the students of the school using specific examples. Clearly articulate why the behavior is *not* acceptable at your school.

3. *Describe the Gap:* Describe the gap between what you expect and what you have observed. End with a clarifying question such as "Am I clear about what needs to happen next?" to check that your expectations are understood.

4. *Make It Motivating and Easy:* Explain the natural consequences of failing to meet expectations, and explore whether the teacher has the skills to be successful. Setting some short-term, attainable goals encourages effort and motivation.

5. *Agree on a Plan and Follow Up:* Agree on specific actions and timelines for follow-up. At this point it is *important* that the plan is both fair and firm, but it is *imperative* to follow through with the plan.

6. *Stay Focused and Flexible:* Continually monitor progress. Check in regularly, and be ready to listen and respond with more or different kinds of support if the circumstances of the situation change.

All principals understand there will be times when they will need to make difficult—even unpopular—decisions or confront teachers about unacceptable behaviors. They recognize that the culture in their schools is only as healthy as the most toxic behaviors they are willing to tolerate. They realize they cannot ignore or condone behaviors that are not aligned with the goal of learning for all. Principals not only accept confrontation as a part of the job; they recognize it as a necessary aspect of a high-performing school and take steps to plan for and manage it successfully.

It has been said that principals have to become comfortable with less than universal love and affection if they hope to be successful in what is, and always will be, a very demanding role. If a principal is the kind of person who needs unconditional love, we recommend that she or he buy a dog, because no matter how difficult the day or how controversial the decision, a dog will always greet you with its tail waging. Principals need to accept that they are never going to receive that kind of affection at school.

MAKING DIAMONDS: TOP-DOWN PRESSURE AND BOTTOM-UP SUPPORT

Last summer a principal shared his frustration with his school's lack of progress implementing PLCs. He said, "It has been drilled into me that if teachers do not buy into an idea, the idea is doomed to failure. But, what if they just don't want to change? Do I force them to become a PLC or be patient and hope they eventually come around"?

This principal's question resonated with me, because for years I had also been told that substantive change must reflect a nearly universal buy-in by the faculty. But what if, as this principal lamented, the faculty liked things just the way they were and did not see the need for change? Should principals wait and hope that some kind of spontaneous enlightenment will come upon the faculty, or should they press forward with what they believe is best for kids regardless of the consequences?

DuFour posed a similar question of principals when he asked, "What drives your school improvement efforts—evidence of best practices or the pursuit of universal buy-in" (2007, p. 1). The answer, according to DuFour, is that "educational leaders must provide both pressure and support if they are to play a role in improving their schools and districts" (2007, p. 3).

If principals intend to shift the culture of their schools from teaching to learning, they must be willing to "make diamonds." Just as diamonds are not created without carbon being subjected to significant pressure deep within the earth, neither is a school's culture changed without significant top-down pressure and bottom-up support from a savvy principal.

> *Educational leaders must provide both pressure and support if they are to play a role in improving their schools and districts.*
>
> —DuFour, 2007, p. 3

Principals must recognize that a part of their role is to exert pressure by clearly and consistently communicating what is important while simultaneously providing the necessary guidance and support of legitimate school improvement efforts. Principals provide that kind of guidance by relentlessly pressing for greater and greater clarity around those practices that benefit student learning.

To appreciate its value, it's important to recognize that top-down pressure need not be conveyed through heavy-handed tactics or overbearing directives. Top-down pressure can more appropriately come in the form of great clarity, careful guidance, and consistent direction by a principal. In fact, the principal who doesn't apply such pressure must recognize that there are costs and consequences in failing to do so. A lack of top-down pressure—as manifested by a lack of clarity about what is important—can result in teachers embracing questionable initiatives that generate only marginal improvements in student learning.

Of course, exerting pressure from the top will be fruitless if the faculty does not have sufficient support to respond to the challenges that the pressure creates. Teachers have a right to expect, even insist, that principals provide the necessary support they need to succeed. Support can take on many forms, such as increased time for collaboration and reflection or specific training sessions on new protocols for data analysis and lesson design.

In PLCs, principals provide the right amount at the right time of the right kind of support teachers need to be successful. They model the behaviors and skills expected from teachers while advocating on behalf of the faculty and staff, as they seek out novel ways of ensuring that all students learn. Richard Elmore (2003) describes this concept as "reciprocal accountability." As principals ask teachers to work together in the implementation of PLCs, so too can teachers expect principals to support them in their work. In a PLC, the relationship works both ways.

Returning to the original question posed by the frustrated principal, we believe successful principals know that meaningful school improvement cannot be achieved by "brute sanity" alone. Change initiatives that rely on compliance are rarely sustainable. Neither do principals embrace "hope" as a strategy to ensure meaningful improvement in student learning. These principals realize they must engage the faculty if they expect to create commitment and lasting change.

The importance of a guaranteed and viable curriculum, common formative assessments, and systematic pyramids of intervention are not up for debate. Working together interdependently on collaborative teams is not optional; it is expected. There has never been a clearer consensus or greater agreement on what schools should do to positively impact student learning. For principals, it is not a choice of pressure or support; it is ensuring that a combination of pressure and support is present in their school.

Principals need not apologize for having high expectations and holding teachers accountable for implementing the big ideas of a PLC. Indeed, given what we know now, it is unconscionable to allow teachers to ignore best practice or sabotage legitimate school improvement efforts that reflect the big ideas of PLCs. It is equally irresponsible, however, to expect teachers to change their practice without the necessary time and support they need to succeed. Clearly stating the expectation that teachers will pursue best practice, while simultaneously providing the necessary support they need to be successful, strikes the right balance.

We are confident many terrific leaders have wrestled with the conundrum presented by the question posed by this principal, but the answer lies in the concept of top-down pressure and bottom-up support. It is this process of making diamonds that ensures our students will have the best opportunity to succeed.

REBOOT THE PRINCIPALSHIP: STRATEGIES TO REKINDLE, REIGNITE, REENERGIZE YOUR SCHOOL

What inspires me is not new ideas, but the obsession with the idea that what has already been done is still not enough.

—Eugene Delacroix

When we first began this book, we were asked why we would want to write another book about Professional Learning Communities. The questions were, "Haven't PLCs been around for a while? Aren't PLCs a tired idea? Why not write about one of the new things people are working on—things like the Common Core and teacher evaluation? Aren't PLCs past their prime, a little passé?"

The question made us reflect on all the conversations we've had with principals about the idea of implementing PLCs to improve their schools. Maybe you have had the same conversations; they often go something like this: "I've heard all that PLC stuff before," or "we already read the PLC book," or maybe "we did PLCs last year."

The initial question begs a larger question: "Why are so many children sitting in classrooms that prepare them for a world that no longer exists?" Why are so many teachers still delivering curriculum that falls miserably short of what is necessary to prepare students for the 21st century? Why do so many children experience pedagogy that fails to ignite their curiosity or engage them in the passionate inquiry of new ideas?"

We wondered: Why it is that so many schools talk about PLCs but continue to engage in practices that were present in schools 30, 40, even 50 years ago? Why are some teachers allowed to ignore the value of a guaranteed and viable curriculum, timely feedback from formative assessments, or providing students with the support they need to learn crucial skills? How can anyone justify teachers working in isolation when the weight of evidence associated with the power of collaboration is so overwhelming? Again, we asked ourselves why and then asked, Is this what we want for our kids?

We have often reflected on these original questions: Are PLCs a tired idea? Are PLCs passé? Is another conversation about leadership in PLCs really just another rendition of the same old song? If it were true that PLCs were so easy to implement, so widely understood, and so thoroughly explored in books and articles, then why were so many schools *still* failing?" In fact, if PLCs were so "yesterday," why are *any* schools still failing? And we accept this reality in our schools—why? Because we have heard all that PLC stuff before? The truth is that there is still a lot of work to be done until every child is learning.

Instead, we turned the questions around and asked them another way. We wondered, Why are so many schools so successful when organized as PLCs? Why were some principals able to overcome significant barriers, while others failed to navigate even the calmest waters without great difficulty? What separates and effective leader from ineffective one? Why are some schools constantly improving, while others are still mired in mediocrity? Why are some schools clearly focused on the singular goal of improving student learning, while others continue to slog through an assortment of fragmented priorities frenetically shifting from one initiative to the next?

Finally, we asked ourselves why so many students in schools functioning as PLCs are experiencing such remarkable success. Why are students in those classrooms demonstrating high levels of growth year after year after year? And why are teachers in those schools reporting higher levels of self-efficacy and satisfaction? What was happening in those schools that embraced PLC concepts?

We believe the answer is because the constructs of effective leadership and concepts of PLCs are so inextricably and irrevocably intertwined with one another. In the hundreds of schools we have visited, we have yet to find a school where leadership was effective that did not embody the big ideas of a PLC. Regardless of what they called it, how it was labeled, or what nomenclature was associated with it, we have found at the heart of any effective school is a principal who embodies the core beliefs of PLCs.

When we are grounded by the optimistic certainty of the power of PLCs, we engage in this work with a passionate belief that we can do better than we have done in the past. Furthermore, when we concentrate on a few, high-leverage strategies that we know will help all students learn, principals can rekindle, reignite, and reenergize their schools around the big ideas of a Professional Learning Community.

Bibliography

Ainsworth, L. (2003). *Power standards: Identifying the standards that matter most.* Englewood, CO: Advanced Learning Press.

Ainsworth, L. (2013). *Prioritizing the Common Core: Identifying the specific standards to emphasize the most.* Englewood, CO: Lead + Learn Press.

Annenberg Institute for School Reform. (2004). *Professional learning communities: Professional development strategies that improve instruction.* Providence, RI: Brown University.

Bland, J., Sherer, D., Guha, R., Woodworth, K., Shields, P., Tiffany-Morales, J., & Campbell, A. (2011). *The status of the teaching profession 2011.* Sacramento, CA: The Center for the Future of Teaching and Learning at WestEd.

Carroll, T. G., Fulton, K., & Doerr, H. (Eds.). (2005). *Team up for 21st century teaching and learning: What research and practice reveal about professional learning.* Washington, DC: National Commission on Teaching and America's Future.

Chokshi, S., & Fernandez, C. (2005). Analyzing Classroom Practice: Reaping the systemic benefits of lesson study. *Phi Delta Kappan, 86*(9), 674–680.

Coe, R. (2002, September 12–14). *It's the effect size, stupid: What effect size is and why it is important.* Paper presented at the annual conference of the British Educational Research Association, University of Exeter, UK.

Darling-Hammond, L., & Bransford, J. (Eds.). (2005). *Preparing teachers for a changing world.* San Francisco, CA: John Wiley & Sons.

DuFour, R. (2007). In praise of top-down leadership. *The School Administrator, 64*(10), 38–42.

DuFour, R. (2013, July 25). Keynote address, PLC at Work Summer Institute, Orlando, FL.

DuFour, R., DuFour, R., & Eaker, R. (2008). *Revisiting Professional Learning Communities at work: New insights for improving schools.* Bloomington, IN: Solution Tree.

DuFour, R., DuFour, R., Eaker, R., & Karhanek, G. (2004). *Whatever it takes.* Bloomington, IN: Solution Tree.

DuFour, R., DuFour, R., Eaker, R., & Many, T. (2006). *Learning by doing.* Bloomington, IN: Solution Tree.

DuFour, R., DuFour, R., Eaker, R., & Many, T. (2010). *Learning by doing* (2nd ed.). Bloomington, IN: Solution Tree.

DuFour, R., & Fullan, M. (2013). *Cultures built to last: Systemic PLCs at work.* Bloomington, IN: Solution Tree.

DuFour, R., & Marzano, R. J. (2011). *Leaders of learning: How district, school, and classroom leaders impact student learning.* Bloomington, IN: Solution Tree.

Durstine, L., & Moore, G. (2003). *ACSM's Exercise Management for Persons With Chronic Diseases and Disabilities.* Champaign, IL: Human Kinetics, as quoted in Ball, D., & Murphy, B. (2008, April).Taking SOAP Notes. IDEA Fitness Journal 5(4). Retrieved from http://www.ideafit.com/fitness-library/taking-soap-notes

Easton, L. B. (2009). *Protocols for professional learning.* Alexandria, VA: ASCD.

Education Resources Information Center. (2009). *The MetLife survey of the American teacher: Collaborating for student success.* New York, NY: MetLife Insurance. Retrieved from http://www.eric.ed.gov/PDFS/ED509650.pdf

Elmore, R. F. (2003). *Knowing the right things to do: School improvement and performance based accountability.* Washington, DC: NGA Center for Best Practices.

Erkens, C., Jakicic, C., Jessie, L., King, D., Kramer, S., Many, T., . . . Twadell, E. (2008). *The collaborative teacher.* Bloomington, IN: Solution Tree.

Evans, R. (1996). *The human side of school change: Reform, resistance, and the real-life problems of innovation.* San Francisco, CA: Jossey-Bass.

Friend, M., & Cook, L. (1996). *Interactions: Collaboration skills for school professionals* (2nd ed.). White Plains, NY: Longman.

Fullan, M. (2005, Winter). The tri-level solution. *Education Analyst—Society for the Advancement of Excellence in Education,* pp. 4–5.

Fullan, M. (2007). *The new meaning of educational change* (4th ed.). New York, NY: Teachers College Press.

Fullan, M. (2008). *The six secrets of change.* San Francisco, CA: John Wiley & Sons.

Fullan, M. (2009). *Motion leadership: The skinny on becoming change savvy.* Thousand Oaks, CA: Corwin.

Fullan, M. (2010). *All systems go: The change imperative for whole system reform.* Thousand Oaks, CA: Corwin.

Gallimore, R., Ermeling, B. A., Saunders, W. M., & Goldenberg, C. (2009). Moving the learning of teaching closer to practice: Teacher education implications of school-based inquiry teams. *Elementary School Journal, 109*(5), 537–553.

Gardner, H. (2006). *Changing minds: The art and science of changing our own and other people's minds.* Boston, MA: Harvard Business School Press.

Goddard, Y., Goddard, R. D., & Tschannen-Moran, M. (2007). A theoretical and empirical investigation of teacher collaboration for school improvement and student achievement in public elementary schools. *Teachers College Record, 109*(4), 877–896.

Goodlad, J. (1984). *A place called school.* New York, NY: McGraw-Hill.

Graham, P., & Ferriter, W. (2010). *Building a Professional Learning Community at work: A guide to the first year.* Bloomington, IN: Solution Tree.

Griffiths, D. M. (2006, March). *Are you drowning in a sea of information? Managing information: A practical guide.* Retrieved from http://www.managinginformation.org.uk

Guskey, T. R. (2010). Formative assessment: The contribution of Benjamin S. Bloom. In H. L. Andrade & G. J. Cizek (Eds.), *Handbook of formative assessment* (pp. 1–40). New York, NY: Routledge.

Hargreaves, A., & Fink, D. (2004). The seven principles of sustainable leadership. *Educational Leadership, 61*(7), 8–13.

Hargreaves, A., & Fullan, M. (Eds.). (2008). *Change wars.* Bloomington, IN: Solution Tree.

Hattie, J. (2009). *Visible learning: A synthesis of over 800 meta-analyses relating to achievement.* New York, NY: Routledge.

Hattie, J. (2012). *Visible learning for teachers: Maximizing impact of learning.* New York, NY: Routledge.

Jacobs, H. H. (1997). *Mapping the big picture: Integrating curriculum & assessment, K–12.* Alexandria, VA: ASCD, as cited in Ainsworth, L. (2003). *Power standards: Identifying the standards that matter most.* Englewood, CO: Advanced Learning Press.

King, M. B., & Newmann, F. M. (2001). Building school capacity through professional development: Conceptual and empirical considerations. *International Journal of Educational Management, 15*(2), 86–94.

Kober, N., & Rentner, D. S. (2011). *Common Core State Standards: Progress and challenges.* Washington, DC: Center on Educational Policy.

Kober, N., & Rentner, D. S. (2012). *Year two of implementing the Common Core State Standards: Progress and challenges.* Washington, DC: Center on Educational Policy.

Kotter, J. P. (1996). *Leading change.* Boston, MA: Harvard Business School Press.

Larner, M. (2007). *Tools for leaders: Indispensable graphic organizers, protocols, and planning guidelines for working and learning together.* New York, NY: Scholastic.

Leithwood, K., & Mascall, B. (2008). Collective leadership effects on student achievement. *Educational Administration Quarterly, 44*(4), 529–561.

Louis, K. S., Marks, H. M., & Kruse, S. (1996). Teachers' professional community in restructuring schools. *American Educational Research Journal, 33*(4), 757–798.

Marks, H., & Printy, S. (2003). Principal leadership and school performance: An integration of transformation and instructional leadership. *Educational Administration Quarterly, 39*(3), 370–397.

Marshall, K. (2006). *Interim assessment: Keys to successful implementation.* New York, NY: New Leaders for New Schools.

Marshall, K. (2008). Interim assessments: A user's guide. *Phi Delta Kappan, 90*(1), 64–68.

Marzano, R. (2009/2010). The art and science of teaching: When students track their progress. *Educational Leadership, 67*(4), 87.

McDonald J. P., Buchanan, J., and Sterling, R. (2004). The national writing project: Scaling up and scaling down. In T. Glennan, J. Bodilly, J. R. Gallagher, & K. A. Kerr (Eds.), *Expanding the reach of education reforms: Perspectives from leaders in the scale-up of education interventions* (pp. 81–106). Santa Monica, CA: Rand.

McLaughlin, M. (1995, December). *Creating professional learning communities.* Keynote address presented at the annual conference of the National Staff Development Council, Chicago, IL.

McLaughlin, M., & Talbert, J. E. (2006). *Building school-based teacher learning communities: Professional strategies to improve student achievement.* New York, NY: Teachers College Press.

Meadows, D. (n.d.). *Leverage points: Places to intervene in a system.* Donella Meadows Institute. Retrieved April 9, 2014, from http://www.donellameadows.org/archives/leverage-points-places-to-intervene-in-a-system/

Meyers, N. J. (2012). *Getting district results: A case study in implementing PLCs at work.* Bloomington, IN: Solution Tree.

Militello, M., Rallis, S. F., & Goldring, E. B. (2009). *Leading with inquiry and action: How principals improve teaching and learning.* Thousand Oaks, CA: Corwin.

Militello, M., Schweid, J., & Carey, J. C. (2008, March). *Si se puedes! How educators engage in open, collaborative systems of practice to affect college placement rates of low-income students.* Paper presented at the annual meeting of the American Educational Research Association, New York, NY.

National Turning Points Center. (2001). *Turning points transforming middle schools: Looking collaboratively at student and teacher work.* Boston, MA: Author. Retrieved from http://www.turningpts.org/pdf/LASW.pdf

Newmann, F., & Wehlage, G. (1995). *Successful school restructuring.* Madison: University of Wisconsin, Center on the Organization and Restructuring of Schools.

O'Connell, P. E. (2001). *Using performance data for accountability: The New York City police department's Compstat model of police management.* Washington, DC: The PricewaterhouseCoopers Endowment for The Business of Government.

Patterson, K., Grenny, J., Maxfield, D., McMillan, R., & Switzer, A. (2005). *Crucial confrontations.* New York, NY: McGraw-Hill.

Pfeffer, J., & Sutton, R. I. (2000). *The knowing-doing gap: How smart companies turn knowledge into action.* Boston, MA: Harvard Business School Press.

Popham, J. (2008). *Transformational assessment.* Alexandria, VA: ASCD.

Printy, S. (2008). *How do principals influence teaching practices that make a difference for student achievement?* East Lansing: Michigan State University.

Quate, S. (2003). *Participant notebook.* New Coaches Seminar: Colorado Critical Friends Group. Front Range Board of Cooperative Educational Services, Denver.

Raywid, M. A. (1993). Finding time for collaboration. *Educational Leadership, 51*(1), 30–34.

Redding, S. (2006). *The mega system—Deciding, learning, connecting: A handbook for continuous improvement within a community of the school.* Lincoln, IL: Academic Development Institute.

Reeves, D. (2002). *Making standards work: How to implement standards-based assessments in the classroom, school, and district* (3rd ed.). Denver, CO: Advanced Learning Press.

Reimer, T. L. (2010). *A study on the principal's role in the development of Professional Learning Communities in elementary schools that 'beat the odds' in reading.* (Doctoral dissertation). University of Minnesota, Minneapolis.

Rick, T. (2012, June 12). Top 20+ mistakes to avoid. [Web log post]. Retrieved from http://www.torbenrick.eu/blog/change-management/top-20-change-management-mistakes-to-avoid

Robinson, V., Lloyd, C., & Rowe, K. (2008). The impact of leadership on student outcomes: An analysis of the differential effects of leadership types. *Education Administration Quarterly, 44*(5), 635–674.

Schlechty, P. C. (1990). *Schools for the 21st century: Leadership imperatives for educational reform.* San Francisco, CA: Jossey-Bass.

Schmoker, M. J. (2001). *Results Fieldbook: Practical Strategies from Dramatically Improved Schools.* Alexandria, VA: ASCD.

Schmoker, M. J. (2002). The real cause of higher achievement. *Southwest Educational Development Laboratory Letter, 14*(2), 3–7

Schmoker, M. J. (2006). *Results now: How we can achieve unprecedented improvements in teaching and learning.* Alexandria, VA: ASCD.

Senge, P. M. (1990). *The fifth discipline: The art and practice of the learning organization.* New York, NY: Doubleday/Currency.

Sergiovanni, T. J. (2005). *Strengthening the heartbeat.* San Francisco, CA: John Wiley & Sons.

Sparks, D. (2004, Spring). Broader purpose calls for higher understanding: An interview with Andy Hargreaves. *Journal of Staff Development, 25*(2), 46–50.

Sparks, D. (2005). *Leading for results.* Thousand Oaks, CA: Corwin.

Stiggins, R. (2007). Five assessment myths and their consequences. *Education Week, 27*(8), 28–29.

Straus, D. (2002). *How to make collaboration work: Powerful ways to build consensus, solve problems, and make decisions.* San Francisco, CA: Berrett-Koehler.

Supovitz, J. A., & Christman, J. B. (2003). *Developing communities of instructional practice: Lessons from Cincinnati and Philadelphia.* Philadelphia, PA: Consortium for Policy Research in Education.

Thurm, S. (2006, January 23). Companies struggle to pass on knowledge that workers acquire. *Wall Street Journal, 247*(18), p. B1.

Tomlinson, C. A. (2007/2008). Learning to love assessment. *Educational Leadership, 65*(4), 8–13.

Turnbull, B. J., Haslam, M. B., Arcaira, E. R., Riley, D. L., Sinclair, B., & Coleman, S. (2009). *Evaluation of the school administration manager project.* (Report for the Wallace Foundation). Washington, DC: Policy Studies Associates.

Valencia, S. W., & Killion, J. P. (1988). Overcoming obstacles to teacher change: Direction from school-based efforts. *Journal of Staff Development, 9*(2), 2–8.

Waters, T., & Cameron, G. (2007). *The balanced leadership framework: Connecting vision with action.* Denver, CO: Mid-continent Research for Education and Learning.

Waters, T., Marzano, R. J., & McNulty, B. A. (2003). *Balanced leadership: What 30 years of research tells us about the effect of leadership on student achievement.* Aurora, CO: Mid-continent Research for Education and Learning.

Watts, G. D., & Castle, S. (1992, April). *The time dilemma in school restructuring.* Paper presented at the Annual Meeting of the American Educational Research Association, San Francisco, CA.

Weaver-Dunne, D. (2000). Teachers learn from looking together at student work. *Education World.* Retrieved from http://www.education-world.com/a_curr/curr246.shtml

Weinbaum, A., Allen, D., Blythe, T., Simon, K., Seidel, S., & Ruben, C. (2004). *Teaching as inquiry: Asking hard questions to improve practice and student achievement.* New York, NY: Teachers College Press.

Wenger, E. (1998). *Communities of practice: Learning, meaning, and identity.* Cambridge, England: Cambridge University Press.

Zemelman, S., Daniels, H., & Hyde, A. (2012). *Best practice: Bringing standards to life in America's classrooms.* Portsmouth, NH: Heinemann.

Additional Readings

American College of Sports Medicine. (2007). *American College of Sports Medicine code of ethics for CSM certified and registered professionals.* Retrieved January 31, 2007, from www.acsm.org/certification/general infor.htm

Birtel, M., & Chilcott, L. (Producers), & Guggenheim, D. (Director). (2010). *Waiting for superman* [Motion picture]. United States: Paramount Vantage.

Blythe, T., Allen, D., & Powell, B. (2008). *Looking together at student work: A companion guide to assessing student learning.* New York, NY: Teachers College Press.

DuFour, R., & Marzano, R. (2009). High-leverage strategies for principal leadership. *Educational Leadership, 66*(5), 62–68.

Fullan, M. (2001). *Leading in a culture of change.* San Francisco, CA: Jossey-Bass.

Koch, R. (1998). *The 80/20 principle: The secret to success by achieving more with less.* New York, NY: Doubleday.

Loewenberg Ball, D., & Forzani, F. (2010). Teaching skillful teaching. *Educational Leadership, 68*(4), 40–45.

Louis, K. S., & Wahlstrom, K. (2011). Principals as cultural leaders. *Phi Delta Kappan, 92*(5), 52–56.

Marzano, R. (2009). When students track their progress. *Health and Learning, 67*(4), 86–87.

Marzano, R. Yanoski, D., Hoegh, J., & Simms, J. (2013). *Using Common Core standards to enhance classroom instruction and assessment.* Bloomington, IN: Marzano Research Laboratory.

McDonald, J. P., Mohr, N., Dichter, A., & McDonald, E. C. (2007). *The power of protocols: An educator's guide to better practice* (2nd ed.). New York, NY: Teachers College Press.

Mourshed, M. (2010, November 29). How the world's most improved school systems keep getting better [Webinar]. Retrieved from http://mckinseyonsociety.com/how-the-worlds-most-improved-school-systems-keep-getting-better/

Mulford, W., Silins, H., & Leithwood, K. A. (2004). *Educational leadership for organisational learning and improved student outcomes.* Dordrecht, the Netherlands: Kluwer.

Myers, N. (2012). *Getting district results: A case study in implementing PLCs at work.* Bloomington, IN: Solution Tree.

Saphier, J. (2005). Masters of motivation. In R. DuFour, R. Eaker, & R. DuFour (Eds.), *On common ground: The power of professional learning communities* (pp. 85–113). Bloomington, IN: Solution Tree.

Schmoker, M. J. (2011). *Focus: Elevating the essentials to radically improve student learning.* Alexandria, VA: ASCD.

The Teaching Commission. (2006). *Teachers at risk: Progress & potholes.* New York, NY: National Council on Teacher Quality.

Index

A SAGE Company